*For my father-Haji Abdul Aziz,
my mother-Hajjah Fathima Hayee,
and my teacher-Glenn D. Paige*

Nonviolence and Islamic Imperatives

Chaiwat Satha-Anand

Ω Irene Publishing 2017

Nonviolence and Islamic Imperatives

by Chaiwat Satha-Anand

(Qader Muheideen)

Professor of Political Science, Thammasat University

Chairperson, Strategic Nonviolence Commission,

Thailand Research Fund

Senior Research Fellow,

TODA Institute for Global Peace and Policy Research

Vice President, Governing Council, Center for Global Nonkilling

Published by Irene Publishing, Sparsnäs Sweden, 2017

Cover Design: Issra Smutkhochorn

Layout: J. Johansen

www.irenepublishing.com

Copyright © Chaiwat Satha-Anand and Irene Publisher

Contents

Preface	7
Chapter I Itroduction: If anyone saves a life…	13
Chapter II The Nonviolent Crescent: Eight Theses on Muslim Nonviolent Actions	33
Chapter III Core Values for Peacemaking in Islam:	57
Chapter IV The Islamic Tunes of Gandhi's Ahimsa	69
Chapter V Muslim Communal Nonviolent Actions: Minority Coexistence in Non-Muslim Society	83
Chapter VI Transforming Terrorism with Muslims' Nonviolent Alternatives?	105
Chapter VII The Jahiliyya Factor?: Fighting Muslims' Cultural Resistance to Nonviolence	147
Legends of chapters	168
Index	171

Preface

Nonviolence and Islamic Imperatives

Imagine the book you are holding in your hand now as a human being. Unlike the introduction which elucidates its architecture, I believe its preface is its biography.

When I finished my Ph.D.dissertation- "The Nonviolent Prince" –a rewriting of Machiavelli's *The Prince* from a nonviolent philosophical perspective-at the Department of Political Science, University of Hawai'i in December 1981, my teacher and mentor - Glenn D.Paige asked me a provocative question: as a nonviolent Muslim, what would I do to deal with the prevalence of violent actions among Muslims in the world? In some ways, this book is my longstanding response to that question. As a collection of essays written at different times beginning with the oldest one in 1986- "The Nonviolent Crescent" (Chapter II), to the latest-"If anyone saves a life…" (Chapter I) in 2015, the book's life spans thirty years- roughly a generation. I could say that I have spent half of my life working on it. This preface is about where each part was born?

Who have helped them grow along the way? And why does it come out as a book at this time?

"The Nonviolent Crescent", perhaps my most cited essay on Islam and nonviolence[1], was born in February 1986 in a Hindu Ashram in Bali- a city that became Indianized twelve hundred years ago. I still remember the warm hospitality of our host, the late Gedong Bagoes Oka-the Gandhi of Bali, together with the energetic support as well as fantastic humor of the head of the largest Muslim organization in Indonesia-Nahdlatul Ulama-the late Abdurrahman Wahid who later became Indonesian President (1999-2001). But it was my teacher- Glenn D.Paige's creative enthusiasm, who envisioned and organized this first conference on Islam and nonviolence, which animated the whole conference. Prof.Ralph E.Crow of the American University of Beirut was also with us in Bali. He was later instrumental in organizing the first Middle East conference on Islam and nonviolence in Amman Jordan in 1987.[2]

"The Islamic Tunes of Gandhi's Ahimsa" was born in July 1990, in another millennial city of Groningen in the Netherlands. It was my contribution to the International Peace Research Association, nonviolence commission. The great Indian editor of *Gandhi Marg*, the late Mahendra Kumar, was there. And he invited me and Glenn Paige, we were then

---

[1] Irfan A. Omar, "Jihad and Nonviolence in the Islamic Tradition," in Irfan A.Omar and Michael K. Duffey (eds.) *Peacemaking and the Challenge of World Religions* (Malden, MA: John Wiley & Sons, 2015), p.29. The essay is considered "indispensable for anyone studying Islam and nonviolence".

[2] The result of the Amman conference was Ralph E.Crow, Philip Grant, and Saad E.Ibrahim (eds.) *Arab Nonviolent Political Struggle in the Middle East* (Boulder: Lynne Reinner Publishers, 1990) "The Nonviolent Crescent" was this book's chapter 3.

convenors of IPRA's nonviolence commission, to publish some papers including "The Islamic Tunes" in a special issue of his famous Indian journal.

With the advent of the first "Iraq war" in the early 1990s, the late Elise Boulding, a pioneer of international peace research, convened a meeting of peace researchers most of whom were with the International Peace Research Association (IPRA) to work on building peace in the Middle East. My "Core values for Peacemaking in Islam" was born in July 1992 in the city of Kyoto, an old capital of Japan for a thousand years. The discussion on peacebuilding in the Middle East was heated and passionate. I have learned so much about the Middle East from friends there, and especially from Elise about the ways she wisely conducted numerous meetings among passionate peace researchers.

"Muslim Communal Nonviolent Actions" was born in Washington DC in November 1998 to address the issues of cultural diversity in Islam and the problematic of religious tolerance. It was both a reunion and a beginning of a long time friendship with several Washington –based academics, many were from American University, a most impressive group of Muslim intellectuals with their critical interests and studies in Islam and nonviolence. Among them were Abdul Aziz Said, Mohammed Abu Nimer, Meena Sharify Funk, Nathan Funk, Ayse Kadayifci-Orellana, and Karim Douglas Crow.

Five years later, and after the horrible terror of September 11, in 2001, the world drastically changed into a security mode with enhanced suspicion if not animosity towards Muslims. Those of us in the fields of nonviolence have serious thought about how nonviolent actions could respond to terrorism.[3]

---

3 For example, Tom H.Hastings, *Nonviolent Response to Terrorism* (Jefferson, North Carolina: McFarland & Company, 2004)

"Transforming Terrorism with Muslims' Nonviolent Action" addresses the spectre of violence, terror, and suicide bombing haunting the world in the name of Islam. The essay was born in October 2003, in the ancient city of Alexandria in volatile Islamic Egypt at perhaps the most exquisite library on earth. I could still recall the fascinating academic discussion by world renowned scholars of Islam who opened up the wondrous world of Islamic studies that at times made me feel both so small and distance from many among those scholars. Despite their kindness to me, there seems to be a sense of reluctance among some to own the idea of Islam and nonviolence represented by the wonderful works such as those by Mohammed Abu Nimer, and perhaps my own.

I have tried to understand such reservations or reluctance to accommodate or at least seriously explore the theories and practices of Islam and nonviolence among many Muslim thinkers and intellectuals. "The Jahiliyya Factor?" was written to come to terms with this problem. It was born in 2004 in another thousand-year-old city of Sopron, Hungary, bordering Austria. I presented this essay at the International Peace Research Association (IPRA), nonviolence commission under the guidance of Prof.Ralph Summy of University of Queensland.

Three decades later, and a decade and a half into the twenty-first century with wars raging in Iraq, Syria, innocent victims of wars and terrors abound. In such a time, "If anyone saves a life…" , the 9th Nurcholish Madjid Memorial Lecture (NMML) of Paramadina Universiti in Jakarta, took me back to Indonesia on October 6, 2015. Apart from the fact that I wished to express my appreciation for the hard works done by my Indonesian colleagues- Ihsan al-Fauzi, Rizal Panggabean, and Irsyad Rafsadi of Pusad Studi Agama dan Demokrasi,

Yayasan Wakaf Paramadina, the lecture gave me a chance to reflect on the late Nurcholish Madjid's contributions to Islam. Nurcholish was my friend and one of the greatest Muslim intellectuals of Southeast Asia. "If anyone saves a life…" retraces the issue of Islam and nonviolence taking into account current literature in the fields of nonviolence and the fast changing global context.

Looking back at the time and places when these essays first appeared, I notice that almost all of these essays were born in cities with more than a thousand years of history - Bali, Kyoto, Groningen, Alexandria, and Sopron, in four continents: Asia, Europe, North America and North Africa. In the past thirty years, many people have seen, read, criticized and enjoyed these essays, with some pieces have even been translated into different languages. Why then do these essays have to become a book?

These essays should come out at this time because the world needs it, perhaps even more so than I first began writing about Islam and nonviolence three decades ago. The Global Peace Index 2016 reports that from 2008 deaths from terrorism increases 286 % killing 32, 715 people all over the world in 2015 including victims in Europe and North America. The majority of terrorist activity is highly concentrated in five countries: Iraq, Nigeria, Afghanistan, Pakistan and Syria. Between them these countries accounted for 78 per cent of deaths from terrorism in 2014.[4] It goes without saying that these are all Muslim countries and many of the terror acts in Europe were carried out by Muslims, called by some as violent extremists. There have been numerous studies trying to explain

---

4 (http://static.visionofhumanity.org/sites/default/files/GPI%20 2016%20Report_2.pdf accessed November 9, 2016)

such reality, some critical, while others apologetic. But until now, interest in the study of nonviolent potentials within Islam is still marginal. The book you have in your hand now does not claim to be a work of Islamic studies. It claims, however, to be a study of nonviolence for Muslims, proving that there is indeed academic ground for Muslims to explore nonviolent alternatives based on Islamic authentic sources that would be conducive to confronting injustice in the world without resorting to violence.

Along the book's life time, many have been kind to it, some embracing it while criticizing it. While it is impossible for me to remember them all, it is the philosopher Suwanna Satha-Anand who has stood by it through thick and thin as my wife and wise critic, while my other teacher- the German philosopher Manfred Henningsen has watched it from the island of Oahu.

The life story of this book, like many others, can be recounted as the story of a manuscript in search of its publisher. Through the years, this one has met with outright rejection, or disinterested acceptance. But it has moved away to search for its home in the house of peace where it belongs. It has finally arrived in the able hands of two fine scholars/activists of nonviolence- Jørgen Johansen and Majken Jul Sørensen of Irene Publisher in Sparsnas, Sweden. I believe that it is the publishers' knowledge and belief in nonviolence as alternatives to change the violent world that help make this book feel at home with IRENE.

Chapter I

Introduction:
If anyone saves a life...

Aylan Kurdi was a three-year old boy. On September 2, 2015, his frail and lifeless body was washed ashore of the Turkish resort town of Bodrum after the ship that carried him and his family away from the wartorn city of Kobani in Syria capsized on the way to the Greek island of Kos. The family was trying to leave Kobani, devastated by the Syrian civil war, besieged by Islamic State for several months which in turn resulted in bombing and street fighting that destroyed much of the city.[1]

The boy has since become a symbol of the refugee situation and those innocent lives victimized by the violence of civil war, especially in the Syrian case.

Though the tragedy of Syria at present cannot be construed without taking into account power politics in the Middle East and the role of great powers, it is tragic because in the final analysis an innocent life such as Aylan's has fallen victim in a needlessly violent world. It is therefore necessary to lessen the

---

1 Lizzie Dearden, A Dusty Burial for the boy who woke up the world, *Bangkok Post*, September 6, 2015, p. 9.

pain of the world by calling for alternative politics that will deal with conflict differently. In fact, that is what had happned in the early days of the present conflict in Syria.

In March 2011, a month after the Tahrir Square nonviolent uprising in Egypt had forced Hosni Mubarak out of his office, some Syrians rose up against the dictator Bashar al-Asad. Children in the city of Daraa sprayed anti regime slogan on city walls, a clear form of nonviolent action. They were arrested, badly beaten and the incident turned into the beginning of a movement against the regime. Citizens of Daraa took to the streets shouting slogans against the regime. Many Syrian mosques served as an assembly point for demonstrators. Informed by Friday sermons against the regime by local imams, nonviolent demonstrations often took place on Fridays. Syrian mosques, some would say, performed an important role especially in the first part of the uprising, not only as places of protest convention, but also in legitimating the calls of the nonviolent protesters.[2]

This book is about a child like Aylan Kurdi and millions other people like him. It is about finding nonviolent alternatives based on Islamic imperatives to conduct politics nonviolently so that their lives would not be senselessly lost to violence, directly and indirectly.

As a peace researcher, I have conducted research in order to lessen violence in the world. Arguing for the limit of violence such as finding ways to restore the sanctity of sac-red spaces- mosques, churches, temples, synagogues, etc., I suggest that in doing so, at least one condition conducive to deadly conflict

---

2 See Frida A. Nome, 'For Regime and Resistance: Islam as a legitimizing Force in the Syrian Uprising", in Sverre Lodgaard (ed.), *In the Wake of the Arab Spring: Conflict and Cooperation in the Middle East* (Oslo: Scandinavian Academic Press, 2013), p. 187.

escalation could be avoided.³ Working on innovative nonviolent actions such as the use of humor, witnessing and cyber nonviolent actions, my colleagues and I have argued that these unusual nonviolent tactics would help expand the sphere of nonviolent methods in dealing with current problems of the world.⁴

As a Muslim peace researcher, I am interested in persuading Muslims to critically explore nonviolent alternatives, based both on inspirations from the treasure of Islamic faith as well as knowledge of how nonviolent actions actually work in the harsh world of politics. The thesis of this book is that: the pursuit of nonviolent alternatives will make it possible for Muslims to hold on to two foundational Islamic principles of protecting innocent lives, such as those of Aylan Kurdi's, while fighting injustice in this world.⁵

This book, *Nonviolence and Islamic Imperative*s, is a product of three decades of research and writing on this subject.

---

3 See for example, Chaiwat Satha-Anand and Olivier Urbain (eds.), *Protecting the Sacred, Creating Peace in Asia-Pacific* (New Jersey: Transaction, 2013).

4 Chaiwat Satha-Anand, Janjira Sombatpoonsiri, Jularat Damrongwithitham and Chanchai Chaisukkosol, "Humour, Witnessing and Cyber Non-violent Action: Current Research on Innovative Tactical Non-violent Actions Against Tyranny, Ethnic Violence, and Hatred," in Akihiko Kimijima and Vidya Jain (eds.) *New Paradigms of Peace Research: The Asia-Pacific Context* (Jaipur: Rawat Publications, 2013), pp. 137-155.

5 This paper is a modified version of the introduction to my book in Bahasa Indonesia. See Chaiwat Satha-Anand, *Barangsiapa Memelihara Kehidupan...Esai-esai tentang Nirkekerasan dan Kewajiban Islam* (Jakarta: Pusad Studi Agama dan Demokrasi, Yayasan Waqaf Paramadina, Paramadina University, October 2015; Jakarta: Mizan Press, 2016-2nd printing)

Nonviolence and Islamic Imperatives

This introductory chapter begins with an analysis of the Qur'anic verse which contains the phrase "If anyone saves a life…" to examine the way saving life is regarded as a prime directive for Muslims. Then the use of nonviolent actions as a kind of weapon in politics will be suggested both in terms of the method's effectiveness compared to the use of violence as well as its unique discriminating quality that would be in line with Islamic imperative on the sacredness of human life. Then the ordering of chapters in this book will be briefly outlined. This introduction concludes with two questions: what would focusing on Islam and nonviolence do to how one sees the world? And what kind of a world would emerge from such visualizing?

"If anyone saves a life…"

The title of this introduction comes from a phrase in a Qur'anic verse. Arguably one of the most quoted verses from *Al-Qur'an* regarding Islam and nonviolence, it is from Surah V (Chapter five, The Feast), Ayah (verse) 32. *The Qur'an* says:

"Because of this did WE ordain unto the children of Israel that if anyone slays a human being-unless it be (in punishment) for murder or for spreading corruption on earth-it shall be as though he had slain all mankind; whereas, if anyone saves a life, it shall be as though he had saved the lives of all mankind."[6]

This complex verse contains fascinating treasures on issues of violence and nonviolence in Islam. First, this verse follows the story of Adam's two sons, Cain and Abel. *The Qur'an* says that when one son threatens to kill another, the brother replied that he will not respond with killing. Cain killed his brother. He

6 *The Message of the Qur'an* Translated and Explained by Muhammad Asad (Gibraltar: Dar Al-Andalus, 1980), p.147.

was filled with remorse and became one of the losers. (V: 27-31)[7] The facts that Abel did not raise his hand against his prospective killer, and that God did not punish the killer with death signifies how complex the response to the issue of killing in Islam is. As a result, *the Qur'an* teaches that slaying (qatala) one human being is equivalent to (like) slaying all humankind while saving one life (ahya) is also equal to saving the lives of all humankind.

Second, while killing and saving one life is equal to doing so to the whole humankind, it should be noted that the weight of "taking a life (i.e. killing)" and "saving a life" is not equal. After pointing to the complexity of the act of killing importantly including the effect of killing on the killer, *the Qur'an* stipulates conditions for allowing such an act: the act of killing will only be possible if the one killed committed murder him/herself or has caused corruption on earth. The conditions stipulated here concerns one of the gravest sins in Islam-murder and causing corruption on earth. On the other hand, the directive to save a life does not have any condition attached. Could one therefore say that the unconditionality of saving a life outweighs taking a human life under certain conditions?

Third, when I look at the Arabic words for "slaying a human being" and "saving a life", I found that *the Qur'an* uses different words. It says "qatala nafsan" and "ahyaha" (saves it) and "ahyan-nas" which are translated as "killing a human being" and "saving a life". But the words "nafs" and "nas" are different because while the former signifies the soul or the desire that is human, the latter means more of a human in the flesh. If one reads this verse back to the story of Cain and Abel in the earlier verses, then when *the Qur'an* says that Cain the killer has become a loser, does it mean that he has lost his soul? Does it

---

7 *Ibid.*, p. 146-147.

say that killing is so grave a sin because in killing another, the killer him/herself will have lost his/her own soul? In a most sophisticated manner, *the Qur'an* is pointing both to the person who has lost his/her life because of the killing and the effect of the act of killing on the killer-he would lose his soul and therefore killing him is not called for.

More importantly is the puzzle that comes with the verse: how can killing or saving a soul or a life equals to the killing or saving the whole humankind? I think this puzzle contains a most unusual quantification problem of a single human life. Unlike Tolstoy's Christian notion of the "Kingdom of God is within you", or the idea of connectedness of all lives in Hinduism which can be readily seen as a basis of nonviolence principle, Islam's principle of nonviolence, I would argue, points to how one human life is equal to the whole of humankind and therefore taking one human life is almost unimaginable unless one is prepared to kill the whole humankind in such an act. To contemplate the meaning of this way of quantification of human life is to construe the ways in which a life is seen in a "web of relationship" with the whole of humanity. That one life is equal to all lives is possible because from a cosmic perspective this is not unlike when one sees a grain of sand which contains the life time of the whole planet earth. To see one life as equal to all lives means, among other things, to be able to see the others as a world in and of him/herself and to also see oneself in that world, especially when "that others" are made to be "the enemy" who perhaps had blood of one's family on their hands. Through such a powerfully enchanted sight, saving one life can be understood as saving the lives of the whole humankind.

This is perhaps why in seeing the picture of a single child- Aylan Kurdi- killed as a result of war in Syria, the task of thinking and acting to save such a life becomes an Islamic imperative for Muslims. It goes without saying that if there were no war in present day Syria, Aylan Kurdi's life would have been saved. Syria had a chance with the use of nonviolent action in the early days of the Arab Spring, but due to a number of factors, it was brutally stolen from the Syrians. To save the innocent life such as Aylan's would mean for Muslims to explore and strengthen the course of nonviolent action as necessary alternative in the conduct of politics.

Nonviolent actions as a weapon

A critical understanding of the power and dynamic of nonviolent actions is crucial for those engaging in violence, Muslims and non-Muslim alike. Anwar Haddam of Algeria's Islamic Salvation Front (FIS) for example, indicated that he believes the only way to bring about justice in Algeria is through violence against the government though its victims include innocent Christian nuns and average Algerians. When asked about armed struggle, he said in an interview: "We don't find any other solution, actually. We are still open for dialogue to find (a) peaceful political solution. But we don't have any other choice."[8] Echoing similar opinion, Muntassir Al-Zayat of the Egyptian Al-Gamaa Al-Islamiyah and Al-Jihad, pointed out that his group chose violence because the Egyptian government closed doors to freedom of expression and political participation. Their violence was the reaction to the government's repression.[9]

Both prominent activists might have felt that it was necessary for them as Muslims to use violence to realize the noble goals

8 Joyce M.Davis, *Between Jihad and Salaam* (London: Macmillan Press, 1999), p. 57
9 *Ibid.*, p. 118

espoused by Islam. However, when stating that there is no choice but to use violence, it is important to take into account what Prophet Muhammad said about the cost of using violence. Jawdat Said notes a famous Hadith (traditions of the Prophet) widely quoted in Islamic literature: "Whenever violence enters into something, it disgraces it, and whenever 'gentle-civility' enters into something it graces it. Truly, God bestows on account of gentle conduct what he does not bestow on account of violent conduct."[10]

Though I discuss the Muslims' cultural resistance to nonviolent action in Chapter VII of this volume, I think it is important to underscore nonviolent action as a viable alternative to the use of violence.

In a most promising work on nonviolent struggle, Kurt Schock points out that: "Nonviolent action refers to non-routine and extra-institutional political acts that do not involve violence or the threat of violence."[11] It may occur through acts of omission, whereby people refuse to perform acts expected by norms or laws; or acts of commission where people performs acts which are not expected by norms or even against the laws. These actions are nonviolent when they do not "threaten or directly result in people forcefully detained against their will, injured, violated, or killed."[12]

Similar to Schock's understanding, I also consider nonviolent action from an instrumental perspective as a weapon for social change and resistance. Understanding its meaning is therefore important to avoid misconceptions about them especially in relation to the common notion prevalent among many Muslim

---

10 Mohammed Abu Nimer, *Nonviolence and Peace Building in Islam: Theory and Practice* (Gainsville: University Press of Florida, 2003), p. 42.
11 Kurt Schock, *Civil Resistance Today* (Cambridge: Polity, 2015), p. 5.
12 *Ibid.*, p. 6.

writers that Islam simply means peace, and that peace and nonviolence are similar, if not identical. In fact, the world's foremost theorist on nonviolent action- Gene Sharp maintains that nonviolent action is quite different from "peace" because it is a powerful means of conducting conflict based on rejection of passivity and submissiveness, and that it does not depend on the assumption that people are good, and that people who use it need not be pacifists or saints, among other things.[13] Comparing violence and nonviolent actions from an instrumental perspective, Schock writes: "Violence works like a hammer, while nonviolence works more like a lever. Through leverage, oppressed and marginalized actors are able to defeat repressive and ostensibly more powerful opponents."[14] What all this means is that nonviolent struggle is a kind of human weapon based on social reality of how conflict works.[15]

In addition, I would like to point out two more important reasons why nonviolent struggle should be a preferred course of actions for Muslims especially those who are fighting injustice in a violent world. First, as a weapon for social change and resistance, nonviolent actions are more effective than the use of violence. In a modern landmark study on nonviolent action analyzing 323 violent and nonviolent campaigns using sophisticated quantitative methods and case studies, Chenoweth and Stephan write that their most striking finding is "that between 1900 to 2006, nonviolent resistance campaigns were nearly twice as likely to achieve full or partial success as their violent counterparts."[16]

---

13 Gene Sharp, *Waging Nonviolent Struggle: 20th Century Practice and 21st Century Potential* (Boston: Extending Horizon Books, 2005), pp. 21-22
14 Kurt Schock, "Introduction," in Kurt Schock (Ed.) *Civil Resistance: Comparative Perspectives on Nonviolent Struggle* (Minneapolis: University of Minnesota Press, 2015), p. 17.
15 Schock, *Civil Resistance Today*, p.5.
16 Erica Chenoweth & Maria J. Stephan, *Why Civil Resistance Works:*

Second, nonviolent actions as a weapon is different from the use of violence in that it is much more targeted and discriminating. Unlike weapons of violence such as military drones which are designed to kill targets and yet collateral damage in the forms of innocent human lives lost often result, nonviolent actions are weapons that can differentiate between a person's roles and his/her activities in life as a human being where no other weapon of violence can. As a result, it is possible for a Muslim nonviolent protester in Jakarta, for example, to boycott a shop that sells goods made by political prisoners in Pakistan, and yet he/she could continue to work with that shop owner at a school fare raising funds for the elderly in the community.[17]

This second point qualitatively differentiates nonviolent actions from the use of violence based on how one should appreciate a human life. If Muslims believe that saving a human life is equal to saving the whole human kind, then aside from the cosmic argument suggested above, the fact that one looks at a human life and sees his/her many roles and functions in life- as a father/mother, teacher/student, worker/ employer, community worker/owner of a factory, means that the totality of a human life as a social being needs to be taken into account. For a Muslim, choosing nonviolent action over the use of violence not only means choosing a more effective weapon but one that is in line with reality of a human life considered sacred by the faith.

The Strategic Logic of Nonviolent Conflict (New York: Columbia University Press, 2011), p.7

17 This is Jørgen Johansen's argument in his "Nonviolence: More Than the Absence of Violence"(2007) cited in Schock, *Civil Resistance Today*, pp.5-6.

The order of chapters in *Nonviolence and Islamic Imperatives*

This book is more than an effort to *Shatter the Myth* that Islam is a religion of the sword[18], or that Muslims have been demonized by Western media.[19] In the past decade, there are four other important books that seem to move in a similar direction with *Nonviolence and Islamc Imperatives* They are: Mohammed Abu-Nimer's *Nonviolence and Peacebuilding in Islam*[20]; Qamar-Ul Huda's *Crescent and Dove* [21] Amitabh Pal's *'Islam' Means Peace*[22]; and Jeffry R. Halverson's *Searching for a King: Muslim Nonviolence and the Future of Islam*[23].

Written by a prominent Muslim scholar on the subjects of peace and reconciliation, Abu Nimer's excellent book reflects a rare Palestinian's perspective with three case studies from the Arab contexts. Relying primarily on Islamic framework, Ul Huda's edited volume is useful as an exploration of the intellectual heritage of Islam, nonviolence and peacebuilding in order to find out what opportunities exist for peaceful changes in the Muslim' contexts. Pal's work, written by an Indian journalist, is a powerful rebuttal against the general misperception about Islam and nonviolence by focusing on

---

18 Bruce Lawrence, *Shattering the Myth* (New Jersey: Princeton University Press, 1998).
19 Farish Noor (ed.), *Terrorising the Truth.* (Penang: Just World Trust, 1996).
20 Mohammed Abu-Nimer's *Nonviolence and Peacebuilding in Islam: Theory and Practice* (Gainsville: University Press of Florida, 2003).
21 Qamar –ul Huda (ed.) *Crescent and Dove : Peace and Conflict Resolution in Islam* (Washington D.C. : United States Institute of Peace Press, 2010).
22 Amitabh Pal, *'Islam' Means Peace: Understanding the Muslim Principle of Nonviolence Today.* (Greenport, Conn.: Praeger, 2011).
23 Jeffry R.Halverson, *Searching for a King: Muslim Nonviolence and the Future of Islam* (Dulles: Potomac, 2012).

the role of tolerant Sufi traditions in Islam and using examples of contemporary Muslim peaceful protests in Kosovo, Pakistan and Palestine/Israel. Halverson is an American professor of Islamic studies from Arizona State University who argues that foundations for nonviolence already exists in Islam, that nonviolent jihad could be seen as an active mode of social transformation, and that there are modern Muslim champions of nonviolence such as Abdul Ghaffar Khan or the Frontier Gandhi, Jawdat Saeed the Syrian thinker, Mahmoud Taha of Sudan, among others, whom he characterizes as the chieftain, the philosopher and the martyr respectively.

Nonviolence and Islamic Imperatives is an attempt to argue that nonviolent actions are in fact the prescribed mode of struggle for Muslims facing present-day deadly conflicts because of Islamic injunctions, both in *Al-Qur'an* and the *Hadiths* (Traditions of the Prophet). These Islamic authentic sources are reinterpreted and empirical cases of Muslims' nonviolent actions, primarily drawn from Southeast Asian context, are analyzed from a critical peace/nonviolence research perspective using the language of philosophy and social science to illustrate the thesis.

In my earlier research, I discussed the ways in which Islam is used to justify violence by looking at works of separatist movements in Southern Thailand. I found that one of the reasons why Islam could be readily used to justify violence is because it is perhaps more action-oriented than any other global religious faiths.[24] Unlike those who maintain that Islam means peace and that the religion has been demonized, I wrote

---

24 Chaiwat Satha-Anand, *Islam and Violence : A Case Study of Violent Events in the Four Southern Provinces, Thailand, 1976-1981* (Tampa: University of South Florida Monograph on Religion and Public Policy, 1990).

The Nonviolent Crescent in 1986 (first published in 1990), which serves as Chapter II in this book, to show that Muslims in the present world are facing a profound dilemma because on one hand, Islam teaches Muslims to fight injustice, yet on the other- the faith prescribes conduct of action permitted to undertake the task of fighting.

It is the thesis of this volume that to overcome this dilemma, nonviolent actions which would allow Muslims to fight against injustice and protect/save innocent lives at the same time is needed. The thesis is supported with a social science reading of Islamic authentic texts from a nonviolence perspective, argue against misconceptions about Islam and nonviolence both from some Muslim quarters and some advocates of nonviolence, confirm the thesis with empirical cases of Muslim nonviolent actions and propose a discussion of how to overcome Muslims' cultural resistance to nonviolence.

Taken as a whole, *Nonviolence and Islamic imperative* is an attempt to argue that nonviolent actions are in fact the prescribed mode of struggle for Muslims facing present-day deadly conflicts.

Chapter II: "The Nonviolent Crescent: Eight Theses on Muslim Nonviolent Actions" argues that because the technology of modern warfare and violent actions transgress limits imposed by *Al-Qur'an* and the Prophetic Traditions, Muslims must adopt nonviolent actions in their struggle for justice. Muslims' potentials for the use of nonviolent actions, eight theses of Muslims' nonviolent actions, could be realized based on their day-to-day religious practices.

Chapter III: "Core Values for Peacemaking in Islam: The Prophet's Practice as Paradigm" analyzes two cases of Prophet Muhammad's practices in solving violent or potentially violent conflicts of his time in order to identify core Islamic values conducive to nonviolent actions.

Chapter IV: "The Islamic Tunes of Gandhi's Ahimsa" highlights a major mistake concerning Islam and nonviolence, evident in a particular sourcebook on nonviolence, which perpetuates the myth of proximity between Islam and violence. Because thousands of Indian Muslims followed Gandhi in the Mahatma's nonviolent struggle for independence, this chapter argues that this was possible because they could trace "Islamic tunes" from within Gandhi's doctrine and practices of Ahimsa.

Chapter V: "Muslim Communal Nonviolent Actions: Exemplar of Minorities' Coexistence in a Non-Muslim Society" argues that through everyday form of participating in conflict situations, Muslims in Thai society who used nonviolent actions in their fights: to defend their communities from drugs; against pathological development; and against greed in fishery, have become much more visible and at times admired by the rest of civil society. Common and different features of these Muslim communal nonviolent actions are also discussed.

Chapter VI: "Transforming Terrorism with Muslims' Nonviolent Alternatives?" argues that terrorism, seen as a form of "political violence"[25], grounded in its own reasons yet producing destructive results to all concerned, needs to be transformed into a more productive/creative conflict with Muslims' nonviolent alternatives. This radical transformation

---

[25] The term "political violence" is used in quotation marks throughout especially in Chapter VI because elsewhere I have argued that "political violence" is a contradiction in terms because violence kills politics. See Chaiwat Satha-Anand, "Violence as Anti-Politics: A Political Philosophy Perspective (April 7, 2014). International Political Science Association, 21st World Congress of Political Science, Santiago, Chile, July 12-16, 2009. Available at SSRN: https://ssrn.com/abstract=2421166 or http://dx.doi.org/10.2139/ssrn.2421166

is possible precisely because of the similarities, not differences, between terrorism used by some Muslims and "principled nonviolence". Existing religious edicts condemning and justifying terrorism by traditional religious scholars as against/supporting the tenets of Islam are critically examined. Examples of Muslims' nonviolent actions as a creative form of resistance aimed and engaged in order to move conflicts in the world towards "truth and justice" are explored as alternatives to religious-based terrorism.

Chapter VII: "The Jahiliyya Factor? Fighting Muslims' Cultural Resistance to Nonviolence" problematizes the notion of "Jahiliyya" (ignorance) as a factor that serves to explain Muslims' resistance to the use of nonviolent actions. This modern "ignorance" is a result of a collective blindness to their own histories of nonviolent actions as well as a common lack of understanding of the theory and practices of nonviolence as effective political actions.

Engaging the world with nonviolence and the Islamic imperatives

Dominique Moisi raises an important question in his *The Geopolitics of Emotion*: what combination of geography, history, religion and culture make Muslims so proud and so ashamed at the same time?[26] One could also venture with him and speculate that for some Christians, maybe it is both fear and hope, and for many Buddhists – longing and letting go? Importantly, he argues that one cannot fully understand the present time without trying to construe the ways in which emotions such as fear, humiliation and hope shape world

---

26 Dominique Moisi, T*he Geopolitics of Emotion: How Cultures of Fear, Humiliation and Hope Are Reshaping the World* (New York: Anchor Books, 2010), p. 124.

politics, and that a clash of emotions between fear in "the West," humiliation in the Muslim world, and hope in East Asia is going on. With his thesis as a point of departure, one might need to ask: in what ways do these feelings contribute to violence and nonviolence in the lives of those who believe in religions? Conditions perpetuating such feeling among Muslims, unfortunately, are prevalent in today's world.

Pal's recent piece on nonviolence and Islam begins with the Americans' perception of Muslims. A 2006 USA Today/Gallup poll revealed that 39 percent of Americans wanted Muslims to hold special identification cards. The same poll found that almost half of Americans feel that Muslims are extremists. Nearly one-fourth would not want a Muslim as a neighbor. Less than half think that Muslims would stand the test of loyalty to the United States. A September 2007 Pew poll discovered that 35 percent of Americans possessed an "unfavorable" perception of Muslims. An August 2007 Financial Times/Harris Poll found that 21 percent of Americans consider the presence of Muslims in their country as a national security threat. An April 2009 Washington Post/ABC poll found that 48 percent hold an unfavorable view of Islam. Nearly three in ten Americans thought that Islam encourages violence against non-Muslims, double such an opinion a year after the devastating terrorist attacks. A USA Today/Gallup poll in March 2011 found that almost three in ten Americans think Muslim Americans to be indulgent toward Al Qaeda, possibly the most reviled entity in the world.[27]

That Muslims are seen as violent by many is not surprising given what has transpired in the present world with the

---

27 Amitabh Pal, "Une Religion de Paix? L'Heritage Non-Violent de L'Islam," *Diogene: Theories et Pratiques de la Non-Violence* 243-244 (Juillet-Decembre 2013), p. 101-102.

increasing speed of modern technology. While most religions possess both violent and nonviolent tendencies, they could be used to legitimize violence when it is seen as necessary to defend the faiths and innocent people or when it is connected with the state when the latter's monopoly of violence overrides and manipulates religious tenets in its service.[28] Some analysts argue, however, that as a powerful legitimizing factor, religions can be a substantive dynamic in bending political conflicts in the direction of active violence or its avoidance. Because religious cultures today are exposed to forms of economic organization, bureaucratic management, high technology, and sometimes angry political discourse, they readily ally themselves with the forces of violence rather than peace and nonviolence.[29] In dealing with religions, it is wise to heed a scholar's caution that: "…every great religion is an ocean, with many bays, inlets, and unplumbed areas; we cannot pour it into a bottle and hold it up to the light. We can only come to it, smell it, taste it, touch it, observe what thrives there and listen to its many moods. Our apprehension of it will be incomplete, but we will not falsify it by reducing it to an image or a model."[30]

However, under the shadow of the September 11, 2001 incident and the threat of violence perceived from the barbarity of organizations such as the Islamic State which has carried out dreadful violence in the name of Islam, there is a dire need for Muslims to engage the world from the perspective of nonviolence and Islamic imperatives. But what does this mean?

---

28 Rachel M. MacNair, *Religion and nonviolence: the rise of effective advocacy* (Santa Barbara: Praeger, 2015), p. 7.
29 See a sophisticated argument along this line in Joseph Chuman, "Does Religion Cause Violence?," in K.K. Kuriakose (ed.), *Religion, Terrorism and Globalization* (New York : Nova Publishers, Inc., 2006), pp. 15-30.
30 John Alden Williams (ed.), *The Word of Islam* (Austin: University of Texas Press, 1994), p.1.

I would argue that it means to critically look at the roles Muslims played in shaping global history through nonviolent actions, and when possible share them with the global public.

Pal, for example, tries to do this by pointing out that Gandhi was influenced by Islam because of his mother's Pranami sect which drew much from Islam. He also points out that Gandhi's first campaign against discrimination towards Asians in South Africa was an attempt to bond Hindus and Muslims together with the Hindu equivalent of jihad, namely satyagraha.[31]

But probing a little deeper into the advent of Satyagraha in South Africa, one might find the secret of nonviolence and the Islamic imperatives that will help Muslims engage the world more creatively. Let me share the story of an alternative 9/11 involving Muslims in the creation of one of the greatest nonviolent experiment in the world.[32]

On August 22, 1906, the Transvaal government in South Africa under the British Empire gave notice of a new legislation requiring all Indians, Arabs and Turks to register with the government. Fingerprints and identification marks on the person's body were to be recorded in order to obtain a certificate of registration. Those who failed to register could be fined, sent to prison or deported. Even children had to be brought to the Registrar for their fingerprint impressions. At the time, there were less than 100,000 Indians in South Africa.

On September 11, 1906, Gandhi called a mass meeting of some 3,000 Transvaal Indians to find ways to resist the

---

31 Pal, "Une Religion de Paix? L'Heritage Non-Violent de L'Islam," p. 111.
32 This story is from M.K. Gandhi, *The Selected Works of Mahatma Gandhi (Vol.3): Satyagraha in South Africa* (Ahmedabad: Navajivan Publishing House, 1997). The quote is on p. 143.

Registration Act. He felt the Act was the embodiment of "hatred of Indians" which if accepted would "spell absolute ruin for the Indians in South Africa", and therefore resisting it is a "question of life and death."

Among these 3,000 people attending the meeting was one Sheth haji Habib, an old Muslim resident of South Africa. Deeply moved after listening to Gandhi's speech, Sheth Habib said to the congregation that the Indians had to pass this resolution with God as witness and could never yield a cowardly submission to such a degrading legislation. Gandhi wrote in his *Satyagraha in South Africa* (1928), that the Muslim went on to solemnly declare that in the name of God he would never submit to an unjust law. Though Sheth Habib was known to be a man of temper, his action on September 11 was significant because of his decision to act in defiance of an unjust law and willingness to suffer the consequences in a spiritually-endowed fight for justice in the name of God.

Gandhi was taken aback by the Muslim's suggestion. He wrote, " I did not come to the meeting with a view to getting the resolution passed in that manner, which redounds to the credit of Sheth haji Habib as well as it lays a burden of responsibility upon him. I tender my congratulations to him. I deeply appreciate his suggestion, but if you adopt it you too will share his responsibility."

On that day, September 11, 1906, in South Africa, the Indian nonviolent movement was born. Gandhi later called his Indian movement: "Satyagraha" or "the Force which is born of Truth and Love or non-violence."[33] This movement went on to free 300 million people from the power of the British Empire and gave the twentieth century a most remarkable demonstration of the power of nonviolent struggle.

---
33 *Ibid.*, p. 151.

But what does it mean more than a century later to "remember September 11, 1906"?

I would say that it means remembering that nonviolent alternative was born in a people's fight against injustice. It means remembering that for Gandhi, it is Truth Force that both binds people together and energize them in their course of struggle against the mighty empire. That is why invoking God as witness in this case reflects the degree to which a person is willing to sacrifice his/her all for "Truth" or God.

Most importantly, remembering the nonviolent 9/11 more than a hundred years ago also means remembering the Muslim role in fostering such an alternative, a practice of nonviolence and Islamic imperatives, at the advent of Satyagraha or Gandhi's nonviolence that later on influence a century of nonviolent struggle around the world which include the American civil rights movement in the US, the 1986 People Power in the Philippines, the 1992 May uprising in Thailand, and the Otpor (Resistance) movement against Milosevic in Serbia 2000, among others.[34]

---

34 Gene Sharp, *Waging Nonviolent Conflict: 20th Century Practice and 21st Century Potential* (Boston: Extending Horizons Books, 2005).

Chapter II

The Nonviolent Crescent: Eight Theses on Muslim Nonviolent Actions

From 1982 to 1984, Muslims from two villages in Ta Chana district, Surat Thani, in southern Thailand had been killing one another in vengeance; seven people had died. Then on January 7, 1985, which happened to be a Maulid day (to celebrate Prophet Muhammad's birthday), all parties came together and settled the bloody feud. Haji Fan, the father of the latest victim, stood up with *the Holy Qur'an* above his head and vowed to end the killings. With tears in his eyes and for the sake of peace in both communities, he publicly forgave the murderer who had assassinated his son. Once again, stories and sayings of the Prophet had been used to induce concerned parties to resolve violent conflict peacefully.[1]

Examples such as this abound in Islam. Their existence opens up possibilities of confidently discussing the notion of nonviolence in Islam. They promise an exciting adventure into the unusual process of exploring the relationship between Islam and nonviolence.

---
[1] *Sanyaluck*: A Reporting and Analyzing Thai Newspaper 7, no. 137 (January 30, 1985).

This chapter is an attempt to suggest that Islam already possesses the whole catalogue of qualities necessary for the conduct of successful nonviolent actions. An incident that occurred in Pattani, Southern Thailand, in 1975 is used as an illustration. Finally, several theses are suggested as guidelines for both the theory and practice of Islam and the different varieties of nonviolence, including nonviolent struggle.

JIHAD

A discussion of Islamic action against injustice is necessarily an examination of one of the most controversial concepts in Islam - jihad. Generally translated as "holy war," the term jihad connotes to non-Muslims desperate acts of irrational and fanatical people who want to impose their worldview on others. But this imposition is virtually untenable because *the Qur'an* says "Let there be no compulsion in religion." In fact, it can be argued that the great Arab conquests were essentially political and ideological. The Muslims were willing to tolerate pluralistic societies, which allowed the tensions of older tyrannies to be relaxed. Islam simply offered many peoples of the seventh and eighth centuries a freer, more secure and peaceful life than they had experienced in the past.[2] Sometimes the conversion process took place in exchange for a Muslim divine's bureaucratic, religious, and educational services. Historically, especially in Southeast Asia, Islam seemed to stress continuity rather than conflict with previous cultures.[3]

What then is the meaning of jihad? Some Muslims considered

---

2 Robert Goldston, *The Sword of the Prophet* (New York: Fawcett Crest, 1979), p. 55.
3 Nehemia Levtzion, *Conversion to Islam* (New York: Holmes and Meier, 1979).

jihad to be the sixth pillar of islam.[4] Among the Muslim legal schools, the Khawarij (seceders) used jihad to impose their opinion on the rest of the Muslim community in the name of transcendent and extreme idealism. They insisted that because the Prophet spent most of his life in war, the faithful should follow his example-that the Islamic state should be organized for war, and heretics forcibly converted or put to the sword.[5] But for Muslims, whose criteria for conduct are the *Qur'an* and the Hadith (traditions of the Prophet), historical examples pale in the face of the Qur'anic verses.

> Fight in the cause of Allah
>
> Those who fight you,
>
> But do not transgress limits;
>
> For Allah loveth not transgressors. (2:190)

According to this verse, aggression is prohibited in Islam, and the fighting that is permitted has its limits. The admonition of other relevant verses provides clarification:

> And fight them on
>
> Until there is no more
>
> Tumult or oppression,
>
> And there prevail
>
> Justice and faith in Allah. (2:193)
>
> Altogether and everywhere. (8:39)

One of the reasons for fighting oppression is

---

4 Hamid Enayat, *Modern Islamic Political Thought* (Austin: University of Texas, 1982), p. 2.
5 John Ferguson, *War and Peace in the World's Religions* (London: Sheldon Press, 1977), p. 132.

> For tumult and oppression
> Are worse than slaughter. (2:191)

In this sense, fighting in the cause of God in Islam is basically synonymous with fighting for justice. The *Qur'an* has a precise injunction to substantiate this point:

> And why should ye not
> Fight in the cause of Allah
> And of those who, being weak
> Are ill-treated (and oppressed)?
> Men, women and children,
> Whose cry is "Our Lord!
> Rescue us from this town,
> Whose people are oppressors;
> And raise for us from Thee
> One who will protect;
> And raise for us from Thee
> One who will help!" (4:75)

There is no need to probe deeper into the exegesis of these verses. For the purpose of this analysis, it can be concluded that jihad means to stand up to oppression, despotism, and injustice (whenever it is committed) and on behalf of the oppressed (whoever they may be). In its most general meaning, jihad is an effort, a striving for justice and truth that need not be violent. According to 'Abd-af-Radhiq's reading of the *Qur'an*, God has instructed the Muslims to propagate their religion only through peaceful persuasion and preaching.[6]

---

6 Enayat, *Modern Islamic Political Thought*, p. 64.

Classical Muslim scholars have placed jihad in three categories. Ibn Taymiya, for example, argues that jihad is achieved sometimes by the heart, sometimes by the tongue, and sometimes by the hand. Jihad of the heart, against one's own weaknesses and inner evil, is often described as the "greater jihad," while the "lesser jihad" is fought against external enemies. Ibn Taymiya also suggests two cardinal rules for jihad by the tongue and by the hand: understanding and patience.[7]

Jihad can be differentiated according to the direction (inner and outer) and method (violent and nonviolent). The inner jihad in the narrowest sense is fought within the individual. In a broader sense, the outer jihad may be seen as a struggle to eliminate evil within the ummah (community). On an even broader reading, jihad can be thought of as a struggle within that portion of humanity that accepts some form of spiritual guidance in order to purify itself.[8] In short, jihad is the command of Allah Almighty and the traditions of Prophet Muhammad that demand a perpetual self-reexamination in terms of one's potential to fight tyranny and oppression-a continual reassessment of the means for achieving peace and inculcating moral responsibility.[9]

The point, however, is not to dwell on the conventional wisdom of separating the concept of jihad into wars and self-purification. What is most important for contemporary Muslims is that jihad categorically places the notion of war and violence in the moral realm. The purpose of jihad, ultimately, is to put an end

---

7 Zaiuddin Sardar, "The Other Jihad: Muslim Intellectuals and Their Responsibilities," *Inquiry* (London) 2, no. 10 (October 1985): 40-45.
8 Gary Legenhausen, "A Sermon on Jihad," *Muslim Students Association of Hawaii Newsletter* 5, no. 6 (January 1985).
9 Munawar Ahmad Annes, "Responsible Strength," *Inquiry* (London) 2, no. 10 (October 1985): 52-53.

to "structural violence."[10] But the means used are not independent of moral scrutiny. On the basis of the *Qur'an* and the Sunnah, rules have been enunciated to forbid Muslims to kill noncombatants. One of the Hadiths reports these instructions by the Prophet: "Go in God's name, trusting in God, and adhering to the religion of God's messenger. Do not kill a decrepit old man, or a young infant, or a woman; do not be dishonest about booty, but collect your spoils, do right and act well, for God loves those who do well."[11] Not only are the lives of the noncombatants deemed sacred, but the *Qur'an* requires that even a tree must be spared:

> Whether ye cut down (O ye Muslims!)
>
> The tender palm-tree
>
> Or ye left them standing
>
> On their roots, it was
>
> By leave of God, and
>
> In order that He might
>
> Cover with shame
>
> The rebellious transgressors. (59:5)

The placing of jihad within the Islamic ethical sphere also means that wanton destruction of an enemy's crops or property is strictly forbidden. This principle was clearly stated in a speech the first Caliph, Abū Bakr, made when he sent his army on an expedition to the Syrian borders:

> Stop, O people, that I may give you ten rules for your guidance in the battlefield. Do not commit treachery or deviate from

---

10 Johan Galtung, "Violence, Peace and Peace Research," *Journal of Peace Research*, 3 (1969): 167-169.

11 James Robson (trans.), *Mishkat al Masabih* (Lahore: Sh. Muhammad Ashraf, 1975), p. 838.

the right path. You must not mutilate dead bodies. Neither kill a child, nor a woman, nor an aged man. Bring no harm to the trees, nor burn them with fire, especially those which are fruitful. Slay not any of the enemy's flock, save for your food. You are likely to pass by people who have devoted their lives to monastic services, leave them alone.[12]

Transgressors of these principles were rebuked. At one time during the conquest, the authorities apprehended a girl who had been publicly singing satirical poems about Caliph Abū Bakr and amputated her hand. When Abū Bakr heard this news, he was shocked and wrote a letter to the muhajir who had punished the girl:

I have learnt that you laid hands on a woman who had hurled abuses on me, and therefore, had her hand amputated. God has not sought vengeance even in the case of polytheism, which is a great crime. He has not permitted mutilation even with regard to manifest infidelity. Try to be considerate and sympathetic in your attitude toward others in the future. Never mutilate, because it is a grave offence. God purified Islam and the Muslims from rashness and excessive wrath. You are well aware of the fact that those enemies fell into the hands of the Messenger of Allah (may peace be upon him) who had been recklessly abusing him; who had turned him out of his home; and who fought against him, but he never permitted their mutilation.[13]

From the verses of the *Qur'an* and these examples from one of the Prophet's companions, it can be concluded that the lesser jihad - the use of physical violence against others-has certain limits. These moral injunctions are possible because Muslims

---

12 Abdul Hamid Siddiqi (trans.), *Sahib Muslim* Vol.3 (Lahore: Sh. Muhammad Ashraf, 1976-1979), p. 940.
13 *Ibid.*

have to practice greater jihad - the process of struggle against worldly passion in oneself. The perpetual inner and greater jihad will guide the conduct of lesser jihad in both its objectives and its conduct. This requirement in Islamic teaching raises the question of whether a lesser jihad can ever be practiced in an age of mass warfare and nuclear weapons.

It is interesting to note that the first symposium in the Islamic world on the nuclear arms race (organized in Karachi, Pakistan, by the World Muslim Congress in cooperation with the University of Karachi in March 1984) was held with the theme "The Nuclear Arms Race and Nuclear Disarmament: The Muslim Perspective." Inamullah Khan, secretary-general of the Organization of the Islamic Conference (OIC) said:

Since 1976, it [the OIC] has addressed itself regularly every year to a consideration of the twin issues of the strengthening of the security of non-nuclear weapon states against the threat or use of nuclear weapons, and of the establishment of nuclear-weapon-free zones...an enunciation of the principles that nuclear disarmament must be universal and non-discriminatory for it to have any sense.[14]

Echoing the same idea, a retired Pakistani general candidly pointed out the frightening capacity of nuclear overkill: "What is worse, there are no signs of reduction in the stockpiles. Instead there is an unbridled race for qualitative and quantitative superiority and more sophisticated weapons are being added to the nuclear arsenal every year."[15] He then suggested that Muslims must make their full contribution to the international

---

14 Proceedings of the World Muslim Congress, Karachi, Pakistan, March 1984. I cannot help but ask if a full-scale war breaks out between any two powers, will any of the "ordinary" states survive?
15 Maj. Gen. Rahim Khan, "Horror of Nuclear War," *Defence Journal* (Pakistan) 10, no. 5-6 (May-June 1984): 13-16.

efforts for general and complete nuclear disarmament. Nuclear-free zones should be established in the Middle East, South Asia, Africa, and other parts of the world, with the ultimate aim being to rid the entire globe of nuclear weapons. States possessing nuclear weapons should extend unconditional and legally binding assurances to refrain from using or threatening to use such weapons against states without nuclear arms. Instead peaceful nuclear technology must be shared among the people of the world. Finally, the Muslims should strengthen themselves through political unity, economic development, and acquisition of necessary technologies, including know-how in the nuclear field.

The argument against nuclear wars and nuclear weapons is fundamental to the question of Islam and violence in the nuclear age. Inamullah Khan argues that although Islam permits fighting, it insists that the use of force be minimal. Furthermore, the Muslim conduct of war must be as humane as possible. A Muslim soldier does not fight for self-glory or plunder, and he is ordered not to kill indiscriminately. Given this mandate, Islam prohibits nuclear weapons because they are weapons of mass destruction and can in no way distinguish between combatants and noncombatants nor between military targets and fields and factories.[16]

It is important to note that this argument is incomplete. Inamullah Khan twice pointed out that "Nuclear weapons are not weapons of war. They are instruments of mass extermination." But the analysis that Muslims are not permitted to use these weapons because they do not conform to the Islamic conduct of violence overlooks an important fact: Nuclear weapons are not the only kind of weapons that cannot

---

16 Inamullah Khan, "Nuclear War and the Defence of Peace: The Muslim View," *International Peace Research Newsletter*, 23, no.2 (April 1985): 9-11.

distinguish between combatants and noncombatants or between military targets and farmers' villages. Khan's omission of this point arises out of an incomplete consideration of the nature of modern warfare.

War casualties have dramatically increased in the twentieth century, which has been characterized as "the century of total war."[17] In its first fifty years over one hundred million people, military and civilian, were killed, and World War II claimed almost thirty-five million civilian lives.[18] This astonishing rate of civilian casualties is basically a result of new technologies such as aerial bombardment, submarine warfare, and chemical/biological warfare.[19] It can thus be said that throughout modern history, especially since the onset of the industrial revolution, technology has had profound implications for the capacity to wage war.[20]

The issue has become more complicated with the proliferation of terrorism. Over the decades, the tendency has been to choose methods that minimize the terrorists' risks. As a result, the targets increasingly have become defenseless victims who have little value as symbols or who are not responsible for the conditions the terrorists say they want to alter.[21] This analysis holds that the critical variables for understanding terrorism are

---

17 See Raymond Aron, *The Century of Total War* (Boston: Beacon, 1955).
18 Francis Beer, *Peace Against War* (San Francisco: W.W. Freeman, 1981), pp. 35-37.
19 Andrew Wilson, *The Disarmer's Handbook* (New York: Penguin, 1983), p. 19.
20 Steven E. Miller, "Technology and War," *Bulletin of the Atomic Scientists* (December, 1985): 46-48.
21 David Rapoport, "Fear and Trembling: Terrorism in Three Political Traditions," *American Political Science Review*, 78, no. 3 (September 1984): 658-677.

not related to technology but rather to the purpose and organization of particular groups and the vulnerabilities of particular societies to them. Nevertheless it is possible to argue that the societies' vulnerabilities more or less depend on the level of destruction of the technology used in terror.

If the effect of terror becomes the prime focus of analysis, then the extent of damage done to human life by modern and sophisticated weapons must be taken into account. In this sense, technology assumes paramount significance.

Michael Walzer points out that one of the hardest questions in the theory of war (or violence in the modern age) is how those victims of war who can be attacked and killed are to be distinguished from those who cannot. The moral quality of war lies, among other things, in the tendency to set certain classes of people outside the permissible range of warfare, so that killing any of their members is not a legitimate act of war but a crime.[22] Perhaps one of the best sets of guidelines for judgment in the conduct of violence includes two major principles: proportionality and discrimination. The principle of proportionality centers on the means of violence. It implies that battlefield use of particularly inhumane weapons should be restricted. The principle of discrimination centers on the objects of violence. It suggests that the belligerents should discriminate between combatants and noncombatants and that noncombatants should be protected.[23]

---

22 Michael Walzer, *Just and Unjust War* (New York: Basic Books, 1977), pp. 41-42. Medieval writers distinguish jus ad bellum (justice of war) from jus in bello (justice in war). "Jus ad bellum requires us to make judgments about aggression and self-defence while jus in bello primarily concerns the observance or violation of the customary and positive rules of engagement." Walzer, p.21.
23 Beer, "Peace Against War", pp. 91-92; Wilson, *The Disarmer's Handbook,* pp. 289-290.

The question is how noncombatants can be protected when the level of violence used is so overpowering that it destroys the possibility of discriminating between combatants and noncombatants. Moreover some users of violence do not intend to discriminate but instead want the terrorization per se to attract attention from the world media so that their causes can be furthered. As a result it is virtually impossible for the innocents to remain safe in an age when the sophistication of modern technology of destruction is coupled with the growing disregard of human life.

Islam does not tolerate such indiscriminate methods. Nor does it allow God's creation-human lives, trees, animals, the environment-to be destroyed. For example, the use of napalm is unacceptable, as are explosions in department stores, hijacking and killing hostages on any means of transportation, and bombing civilian targets. The modern world has made primitive weapons obsolete, but the encompassing moral sphere of Islam also renders modern weapons morally illegitimate. Does this conflict mean that oppressed Muslims should submit and ignore the command of God to fight? Is there any alternative for Muslims in the contemporary world? Before these questions can be discussed, Islamic ideas and teachings conducive to the absence of violence should first be appreciated.

ISLAM AND THE PROMOTION OF LIFE

In the Beginning, Allah Almighty said:

> Behold the Lord to the Angels,
>
> "I will create a vicegerent on earth." (2:30)

God created people to be the vicegerents on earth and instilled

His spirit in every man, woman, and child.

> When I have fashioned him
> (In due proportion) and breathed
> Into him of My spirit,
> Fall ye down in obeisance
> Unto him. (15:29)

This verse suggests the sacredness of human life because the spirit of the Creator resides within the otherwise empty body. In this sense, also, humankind is one.

> Mankind was one single nation,
> And Allah sent Messengers
> With glad tidings and Warnings. (2:213)

The unity of humankind is asserted repeatedly in the *Qur'an*.

> Mankind was but one nation,
> But differed (later). Had it not
> Been for a Word
> That went forth before
> From thy Lord, their differences
> Would have been settled
> Between them. (10:19)

Once these verses are appreciated, then it is possible to understand the meaning of a verse such as this:

> And if anyone saved a life,
> It would be as if he saved
> The life of the whole people. (5:32)

Human life is thus sacred. Humankind is one single family, and every human life has a value equivalent to the sum total of all human lives.

Murder is considered one of the four major sins in Islam.[24] Yet there is a paradox: If Islam values the sanctity of life, how can Muslims fight "tumult and oppression" to the end? Unless Muslims forsake the methods of violence, they cannot follow the seemingly contradictory injunctions. It is evident that fighting against injustice cannot be avoided. But the use of violence in such fighting can be eschewed. Alternatives to violence must be adopted if the sanctity of life is to be preserved. Because nonviolent alternatives do exist,[25] an argument can be made that for Muslims to be true to their faith, they have no alternative but to utilize nonviolent action in the contemporary world. The question then is whether Islam embodies conditions conducive to the use of effective nonviolent actions.

NONVIOLENT ACTION AS AN ISLAMIC MODE OF STRUGGLE

What is needed to practice nonviolent action? Gandhi answers:

> *Belief in non-violence is based on the assumption that human nature in its essence is one and therefore unfailingly responds to the advances of love... The non-violent technique does not depend for its success on the goodwill of the dictators, for a non-violent resister depends on the unfailing assistance of God which sustains him throughout difficulties*

---
24 Robson, *Mishkat al Masabhih*, p. 16.
25 Gene Sharp, *The Politics of Nonviolent Action* (Boston: Porter Sargent, 1973).

> *which could otherwise be considered insurmountable.*²⁶

In another place, he writes:

Truth and non-violence are not possible without a living belief in God, meaning a self-existent, all-knowing, living force which inheres in every other force known to the world and which depends on none, and which will live when all other forces may conceivably perish or cease to act.²⁷

A Muslim following Gandhi's teaching would not feel estranged. In fact, it may be possible to trace the Islamic influence on Gandhi concerning the omnipotent and incomparable God. Faith in the supreme Allah already exists in the hearts of every true Muslim.

If Gandhian nonviolence is not sufficient, a modern theory of power may suffice. Gene Sharp writes:

> *Political power disintegrates when the people withdraw their obedience and support. Yet, the ruler's military equipment may remain intact, his soldiers uninjured, the exiles unscathed, the factories and transport systems in full operational capacity, and the government buildings undamaged. But everything is changed. The human assistance which created and supported the regime's political power has been withdrawn. Therefore, its power has disintegrated.*²⁸

For Muslims, this so-called modern theory of power simply embodies the basic Islamic principle that a person should submit only to the Will of God. As a result, a Muslim is not

---
26 Mohandas K. Gandhi, *Non-violence in Peace and War* Vol. I (Ahmedabad: Navajivan Publishing House, 1948), p. 175.
27 *Ibid.*, p. 112.
28 Sharp, *The Politics of Nonviolent Action*, pp. 63-64.

bound to obey anyone whose power has been used unjustly. The *Qur'an* gives the following warning:

> When (at length) the order
>
> For fighting was issued to them,
>
> Behold a section of them
>
> Feared men as-
>
> Or even more than-
>
> They should have feared Allah. (4:77)

Yet there is assurance as well:

> Behold! Verily on the friends
>
> Of God there is no fear,
>
> Nor shall they grieve. (10:62)

Complete submission to the Will of Allah means that if Muslims are oppressed and too weak to fight back, they nevertheless must refuse to obey an unjust ruler. They do have a means to refuse-they can leave. And leave they must, because the command of God on this issue is quite clear.

> When angels take
>
> The souls of those
>
> Who die in sin
>
> Against their souls,
>
> They say: "in what (plight)
>
> Were ye?" They reply:
>
> "Weak and oppressed
>
> Were we in the earth."

They say: "Was not

the earth of Allah

Spacious enough for you

To move yourselves away

(From evil)?" (4:97)

Whether Muslims are weak or strong, they must do something, and it is this tendency toward action that enables them to engage easily in nonviolent struggle. As a technique, nonviolent action is not passive: "It is not inaction. It is action that is nonviolent."[29] Hence, by definition, nonviolent action cannot occur except by the replacement of passivity and submissiveness with activity, challenge, and struggle.

NONVIOLENT ACTION OF PATTANI, 1975

The proximity between Islam and nonviolence can be illustrated with a case study. On November 29, 1975, five adult Malay Muslims and a thirteen-year-old boy traveling in Narathiwat, southern Thailand, were stopped and put into a dump truck by a group of people dressed in dark green suits. When the truck reached the Kor Tor bridge separating Narathiwat from Pattani, the six civilians were stabbed in the back, their skulls crushed, and their bodies thrown into the river. Fortunately, the boy survived, and the massacre was brought to public attention by a group of Muslim activists who began a protest.[30]

---

29 *Ibid.*, pp. 64-65.
30 Chaiwat Satha-Anand, *Islam and Violence: A Case Study of Violent Events in the Four Southern Provinces of Thailand 1976-1981* (Tampa, Florida: University of South Florida monograph on Religions and Public Policy, 1987, 2nd printing 1990).

The people started their peaceful demonstration on December 12, 1975, in the compound of the central government house in Pattani, then formed the Civil Rights Protection Center to keep the protest going. On behalf of the Muslims, the center issued four demands to the government: the arrest of the criminals by rule of law, compensation for the victims' families, withdrawal of government troops within seven days, and a meeting by December 16 between Prime Minister M. R. Kukrit Pramoj and the people. The government did not seem to take these demands seriously, but the Muslims persevered.

On December 13, 1975, university students from institutions in the south came to join the protest. The military and the police surrounded the city of Pattani. During a panel discussion that evening, a bomb exploded among the people. One of the coordinators of the protest rushed to the microphone shouting "Do not flee!" He was fatally shot on the stage. The police came and put an end to the protest. There were twelve deaths and more than thirty people injured, seven of whom were women and children.

This incident caused the people grave concern and sadness. On the same day, around fifty thousand gathered again at the central mosque in Pattani, patiently braving the torrential rain. In retaliation, schools in Pattani and Narathiwat were burned, and the people accused the soldiers of committing arson. One more officer of the Civil Rights Center was stabbed to death. The government did not yield-but neither did the people. On December 21, Muslims from Bangkok rallied at their central mosque to pray for those killed. On the following day, nine educational institutions joined the protest by suspending classes.

The government responded by saying that the protest was but a minor incident involving only a few hundred people, a claim that prompted a huge demonstration on December 28. The mass of people formed themselves into a parade more than three kilometers long, marching in orderly fashion with Thai flags and portraits of the Thai king and queen leading their procession. Even a heavy rain could not weaken their will as they walked toward the Toh Ayah graveyard. The organizers pointed out that this demonstration was an attempt to fight for justice, display the people's strength, and demonstrate that the protest was not the "minor" incident the government claimed it to be. The protesters prayed for the souls of the deceased and then dispersed at 6:00 p.m.

On January 2, 1976, Thai Muslim government officials from the five southern provinces met to consider how to encourage the Prime Minister to come to Pattani. They announced on January 4 they would strike on the following day if their demands were not met. On January 10 their representatives met with the prime minister, who promised to go to Pattani. The protest ended after forty-five days with, among other things, the removal of Pattani's governor and his replacement by a Muslim.[31]

There seem to be five conditions that enabled the Muslim protesters to stage a sustained nonviolent protest in Pattani. First, they possessed the will to disobey, without which no nonviolent action can be realized. The Muslims are willing to disobey because for them God alone is supreme. This total submission to Allah in turn means a rejection of any other form of absolute authority, including the state's.

Second, the Pattani Muslims were courageous despite severe repression by the state apparatus. Because they submitted to Allah alone, they did not have to fear any mortal. Muslims

---

31 *Thai Rath* (Thai daily paper), December 13, 1975-January 26, 1976.

believe as a precept of iman (faith) that all the good and bad incidents in their lives are bestowed upon them by God. As a result, resignation while working for a just cause, without fear of punishment, becomes possible. In the final analysis, they believe God will take care of them.

Third, Muslim discipline enabled the gathering, the protest march, and even the threat to resign en masse to be carried out efficiently. All of the activities were well orchestrated. The quality of discipline bears little relationship to the leadership of the group because it takes time to cultivate such a collective trait. Muslims, however, are already disciplined in their everyday life; that they pray five times a day contributes to this quality.

Fourth, the concept of ummah (community) is very strong among Muslims, who find this unity of brotherhood expressed in the *Qur'an*:

>And hold fast
>
>All together, by the Rope
>
>Which God (stretches out
>
>For you) and be not divided
>
>Among yourselves. (3:103)

Fifth, the feeling among the Pattani Muslims was anything but passive. Islam repeatedly encourages action, and although jihad can be performed by the heart, the tongue, or the hand, the important requirement is that it be performed in one way or another. It is also important to note that two out of three ways of performing jihad are action-oriented. Action, therefore, is of paramount importance for Muslims, just as it is at the core of the modern theory of nonviolence.

These five characteristics of the Muslims evident in the Pattani case can be termed the "Five Pillars of Muslim Nonviolent Action." Interestingly they correspond well with the sacred Five Pillars of Islam: shahadat (a vow that proclaims there is no god but God and Muhammad is His messenger); salāt (prayers at specific times five times a day from sunrise to sunset, each preceded by proper ablution); zakah (compulsory religious tax that every Muslim has to pay); sawm (fasting in the month of Ramadān every year by abstaining from food and drink from sunrise to sunset while purifying both the tongue and the heart in the process); and hajj (pilgrimage to the holy city of Mecca at least once in a lifetime if one can afford it).

Each of these five pillars produces a special quality for those who continually practice them. The shahadat vow by a Muslim is an act asserting that the person will not allow other things to supersede the Will of God. This obedience to God entails the possibility of disobedience to any power that contradicts God's command. The salāt, at a lower level of understanding, is an exercise in disciplinary action. When offered in a congregation, which is usually encouraged, it becomes an assertion of equality because the poor can stand shoulder to shoulder with the rich in such a prayer. The zakah reminds Muslims of their obligation to society at large because the tax sensitizes them to the problems of others and induces them to do something about it. The sawm, both a lesson of self-sacrifice and empathy, enables Muslims to develop patience, the quality that Abdul Ghaffar Khan, the leader of the nonviolent struggle by the Pathans against the British, regards as crucial for nonviolence in Islam.[32] Finally, the hajj is a reaffirmation of brotherhood and the belief that all Muslims form one nation, regardless of race, color, nationality, or class. It is a return to the beginning,

---

32 Eknath Easwaran, A *Man to Match His Mountains: Badshah Khan, Nonviolent Soldier of Islam* (Petaluma, CA: Nilgiri Press, 1985), p. 117.

an immersion in the eternal source of life that has guided their ancestors for millennia.

In other words, a practicing Muslim should possess the potentials for disobedience, discipline, social concern and action, patience and willingness to suffer for a cause, and the idea of unity-all of which are crucial for successful nonviolent action.[33] It remains to be seen how Muslim intellectuals will attempt to tap the fertile resources of nonviolent thought within their own tradition and resolve the paradox of living as a true Muslim in the contemporary world.

CONCLUSION

This chapter has attempted to address Muslims and others interested in the relationship of Islam to the modern world. The points of reference made here are primarily sources most Muslims accept-the *Qur'an* and the Hadith. It is indeed essential that Islam is looked at from a fresh angle. Because the conventional worldview accepts violence as normal, a nonviolent Muslim must part with this paradigm. To have a paradigm shift, the fundamental acceptance of violence must be seriously questioned.

The eight theses on Muslim nonviolent action that follow are suggested as a challenge for Muslims and others who seek to reaffirm the original vision of Islam so that the true meaning of peace-the absence of both structural as well as personal violence-can be obtained:

1. For Islam, the problem of violence is an integral part of the Islamic moral sphere.

---

33 Sharp, *The Politics of Nonviolent Action*, Parts 1 and 2.

2. Violence, if any, used by Muslims must be governed by rules prescribed in *the Qur'an* and Hadith.

3. If violence used cannot discriminate between combatants and noncombatants, then it is unacceptable in Islam.

4. Modern technology of destruction renders discrimination virtually impossible at present.

5. In the modern world, Muslims cannot use violence.

6. Islam teaches Muslims to fight for justice with the understanding that human lives-as all parts of God's creation- are purposive and sacred.

7. In order to be true to Islam, Muslims must utilize nonviolent action as a new mode of struggle.

8. Islam itself is fertile soil for nonviolence because of its potential for disobedience, strong discipline, sharing and social responsibility, perseverance and self-sacrifice, and the belief in the unity of the Muslim community and the oneness of humankind.

That such theses of Muslim nonviolent action are essential to peace in this world and the true meaning of Islam is evident from the *Qur'an*:

> Peace!-a Word
>
> (of salutation) from the Lord
>
> Most Merciful! (36:58)

Chapter III

Core Values for Peacemaking in Islam: The Prophet's Practice as Paradigm

As a *deen*, or comprehensive way of life, Islam claims to encompass all spheres of human activities. Therefore, it is not difficult to search for the concepts of peacemaking from within the faith. However, to identify "core values" conducive to peacemaking that are generally acceptable among the Muslims can be more difficult because in Islam the notion of peace itself is not unproblematic. For example, some would argue that the famous Arabic word for peace, *salam,* denotes only the sense of tranquility and salvation, whereas the term *sulh,* which means truce or armistice, denotes the ending of war.[1] Others would maintain that the word *salam* has at least six meanings, which include an unworldly sense of security and permanence, soundness, preservations/salvation, salutation, resignation

---

[1] Bernard Lewis, *The Political Language of Islam* (Chicago: The University of Chicago Press, 1991), pp. 78-79. Lewis also indicated that according to the jurists, the permanent relationship between the world of Islam and the world of unbelievers was one of open or latent war. If this line of thought is uncritically accepted, then it will not be possible to talk about peace or peacemaking in Islam.

without discontentment, and freedom from jarring elements.²

In order to arrive at core values conducive to peacemaking that will be highly acceptable by most Muslims, Prophet Muhammad's peaceful practices in solving violent or potentially violent conflicts will be suggested and core values identified from these practices. Since his practice (*Sunnah*) is already accepted as a paradigm for human affairs among Muslims, the process of highlighting these core values will contribute much to peacemaking approaches to existential situations in which Muslims are parties in violent conflicts. I will begin with a brief clarification on the notion of peacemaking.

PEACEMAKING

The International Peace Research Association, in its 1990 report to UNESCO on "Peace Building and Development in Lebanon," distinguished "peace building" from "peacekeeping" and "peacemaking." Peace building is considered a confidence-building measure aiming to reduce misperceptions and stereotypes. It also facilitates improved relations by encouraging conflicting parties to participate in joint programs.³ Johan Galtung maintained that peacekeeping, peacemaking and peace building belong to different approaches. Peacekeeping, generally related to military endeavor, is dissociative. Whereas peacemaking arises from the conflict resolution approach, peace building is considered associative. He seemed to favor peace building because it turns toward "deeplying factors" in

---

2 *The Glorious Quran*, A. Yusuf Ali (trans.) (The Muslim Students' Association of the United States & Canada, 1977), p. 780, fn. 2512. All Quranic verses cited in this chapter come from this source.

3 International Peace Research Association, "Peace Building and Development in Lebanon," a final report submitted to UNESCO, Paris, April 11-13, 1990, pp. 7-8.

the relation between the parties and it focuses on "peace structures" that remove causes of war and offer alternatives to war in potentially violent situations. Galtung, however, acknowledged the fact that the idea of peace building is perhaps "too structural and does not take sufficiently into account the importance of attitudes, sentiments, emotions."[4] But he argued that peacemaking, with its emphasis on the actors and their sense of moral obligation and commitment, "is generally not enough."[5]

In the context of searching for core values conducive to peace from within religious traditions, I would argue that the notion of peacemaking should be called for precisely because of its emphasis on "attitudes, sentiments, emotions, and moral obligations." Peacemaking strongly connotes human doing. People *make* friends but they *build* a B-52 or a nuclear submarine. If peace is to be conceptualized humanly, as an absence of both direct and structural violence, and if structures can be created humanely through human actions, then the term peacemaking should be chosen.

Peacemaking has also been used in relation to nonviolent actions. In discussing transformative efforts toward an unarmed mode of action, Beverly Woodward defined nonviolent peacemaking as "various kinds of unarmed intervention in violent or potentially violent conflict situations."[6]

---

4 Johan Galtung, "Three Approaches to Peace: Peacekeeping, Peacemaking, and Peacebuilding," in Johan Galtung, *Peace, War and Defence: Essays in Peace Research* (Vol. II) (Copenhagen: Christian Ejlers, 1976), 302.
5 *Ibid.*, pp. 296-297.
6 Beverly Woodward, "Nonviolent Struggle, Nonviolent Defense and Nonviolent Peacemaking," in Carolyn M. Stephenson (ed.), *Alternative Methods for International Security* (New York: University Press of America, 1982), p. 141.

This type of activity is guided by "the twin goals of reducing violence and protecting the rights of the various parties to the conflict." [7] Moreover, the term peacemaking also has its religious connotation. "Blessed are the peacemakers" is a well-known Biblical verse from the Sermon on the Mount.[8]

For my purposes, peacemaking, with its strong human emphasis, is most appropriate here because it will be from the life and practices of Prophet Muhammad that the desirable core values will be identified.

PROPHET MUHAMMAD'S PRACTICES AS A PARADIGM OF MUSLIMS' VALUES

Muslims believe that the *Qur'an* is God's Word revealed through the unlettered Prophet Muhammad. The Prophet must be unlettered for the same reason that Mary, Mother of Jesus, must be virgin. This is because the Divine Word can only be written on the pristine and pure ground of human receptivity. "If this Word is in the form of flesh the purity is symbolized by the virginity of the mother who gives birth to the Word, and if it is in the form of a book this purity is symbolized by the unlettered nature of the person who is chosen to announce this Word."[9]

In this sense the Prophet's life and actions reflect the Divine message revealed through him. Imam Al-Gazzali (1058-1111), one of Islam's greatest theologians and philosophers, wrote that

---

7 *Ibid.*, p. 148, fn. 5
8 *The New Jerusalem Bible*, Mathew 5:9 (London: Darton, Longman & Todd, 1985), p. 1616.
9 Seyyed Hossein Nasr, *Ideals and Realities in Islam* (London: Unwin Hyman, 1988), p. 44.

the Prophet's character is the *Qur'an*.[10] This is why the *Qur'an* says: "Ye have indeed in the Apostle of God [Muhammad] a beautiful pattern [of conduct]."[11] His life constitutes a universal example for Muslims all over the world. And because he participated in social and political life in its fullest sense, his conduct encompasses all spheres of human activities.

I will focus on two important incidents where the Prophet's peacemaking activities were quite evident. These two incidents, well known among Muslims all over the world and therefore generally accepted, are the rebuilding of Ka'ba in 605 and the victorious return to Mecca in 630. Although historically unrelated, they are theoretically linked, especially when viewed from a peacemaking perspective. The first took place before the *Qur'an* was revealed to him and therefore it was the time when he could be considered a common person without any ruling power. It was also a potentially violent conflict. The second took place when he returned to Mecca as a victor and a powerful political leader after a long exile in Medina. This incident could be considered the final phase of a prolonged violent conflict. Core values conducive to peacemaking can be identified from his actions in both incidents, performed first as an ordinary individual and later a powerful political leader.

THE REBUILDING OF KA'BA

According to the *Qur'an*, the Ka'ba was built by Abraham[12] as the first House of God in the traditions of monotheism. In the Ka'ba, there is a black stone that is believed to be a meteor. Al-Gazzali wrote that the black stone "is a jewel out of the

---

10 Imam Al-Gazzali, *Ihya Ulum-id-Din*, Maulana Fazul-ul-Karim (trans.), (Lahore: Sind Sagar Academy, n.d.), Book II, p. 260.
11 *Al-Qur'an*, XXX: 21.
12 *Al-Qur'an*, II: 125-127.

jewels of Paradise."¹³ In the Islamic tradition, this stone from heaven symbolizes the original covenant (*al-mithaqa*) between God and human beings and that the latter have to live in accordance with truth and take care of the earth.¹⁴

In the year 605, when Prophet Muhammad was thirty-five, the people of Mecca were rebuilding the Ka'ba, which had been destroyed earlier by flood. As it then stood it was without a roof and was merely above the height of a man. Different clans gathered stones to increase the height of the building. They worked separately until the walls were high enough to place the black stone in its corner. Then there was an explosive disagreement because each clan wanted the honor of lifting it into its place. The deadlock lasted for four or five days and the clans prepared for battle to resolve the conflict.

Then the eldest man present proposed to the conflicting parties to heed the advice of the next man to enter the precinct surrounding the Ka'ba through the gate "Babas Safa." They all agreed. The first man who walked through that gate was Muhammad. Everyone was happy because Muhammad was known among them as *Al-Amin,* the trustworthy and the faithful one. They were prepared to accept his judgment.

After listening to the case, Muhammad asked them to bring him a cloak, which he then spread on the ground. He took up the black stone and laid it in the middle of the garment. Then he said, "Let each clan take hold of the border of the cloak. Then lift it up, all of you together." When they raised it to the proper height, he took the stone and placed it in the corner himself. And the rebuilding of the Ka'ba continued until its completion.¹⁵

---

13 Al-Gazzali, *Ihya Ulum-id-Din*, Book I, p. 234.
14 Nasr, *Ideals and Realities in Islam*, p. 26.
15 Martin Lings, *Muhammad*: *His Life Based on the Earliest Sour-*

From his action in this case, the following core values for peacemaking can be identified. Patience is certainly a major value in his peacemaking effort because first he listened. The act of listening signifies his patience and willingness to learn all the information he could. By asking each clan to hold on to the border of the cloak he was affirming the significance and dignity of each of the conflicting parties. They were all equal. A core value here is the respect for the humanity of all parties. When he asked them to lift the cloak together, his action implied that honor needs not be acquired at the expense of dishonoring others or by using violence, it can be shared. In fact, the value of sharing is of paramount importance in this case. Sharing is made possible by equal participation among conflicting parties. In addition, the value of creative thinking signified by the innovative use of the cloak as a vehicle for solving this conflict must also be underscored.

Taken together, the paradigm of peacemaking derived from the Prophet's action at the time when he was without any official political power is constituted by four significant values: patience, respect for the humanity of all, sharing, and creativity in problem solving.

THE RETURN TO MECCA

The Divine Message was first revealed to the Prophet when he

---

ces (Rochester, Vt.: Inner Traditions International, Ltd., 1983), pp. 41-42. The life of the Prophet is documented in the Hadith, the authenticity of which some scholars may question. This chapter is not a place to assess the level of authenticity of the sources of the incidents cited here. The point, however, is that a story in the life of the Prophet such as this one is popular. The two incidents are primarily chosen for their pedagogical value and relevance to peacemaking efforts in the minds of the Muslims in general.

Nonviolence and Islamic Imperatives

was forty. After some time the powerful in Mecca felt that his message was a threat and tried to dissuade him from preaching. Many of his followers were persecuted. Some were tortured and killed.[16] In 622, when he was fifty-three, the Prophet led the Muslims in an exodus from Mecca to Medina known as the *Hijrah*. After eight years of struggles and battles with the Meccans, he led an army of ten thousand men back to Mecca. The Meccans who had wronged the Muslims in the past were afraid of revenge.

But once he entered the city of Mecca, the Prophet addressed the people waiting not far from the Ka'ba. He asked: "What say ye, and what think ye?" They answered: "We say well and we think well: a noble and generous brother, son of a noble and generous brother. It is thine to command." He then spoke to them in the words that, according to the *Qur'an*, were Joseph's when he forgave his brothers who came to him in Egypt. He said: "Verily I say as my brother Joseph said: This day let no reproach be [cast] on you: God will forgive you, And He is the Most Merciful of those who show mercy." [17]

It seems evident that the single most important value that can be identified from the Prophet's action at the time of his conquest of Mecca is forgiveness. This action was not merely a political expedient because if follows an established pattern of conduct. Al-Gazzali recounted that once a man raised a sword over the Prophet's head and asked who would protect him. Prophet Muhammad answered: "God." The sword fell from the man's hand and the Prophet picked it up. He then asked the man to bear witness that there is no deity but God and that Muhammad is His messenger. The man said: "I have got no envy against you, I shall not kill you. I shall not go with

---

16 *Ibid.*, pp. 79-80.
17 *Al-Quran*, XII: 92. See the details of the Prophet's return to Mecca in Lings, *Muhammad*, pp. 297-303.

you and I shall not join those who fight against you." Then the Prophet set him free.[18] In another case a Jew mixed poison in the food of the Prophet at Khaiber. When the woman was caught, she said: "I intended to kill you." The Prophet responded that, "God will not give you that power." His companions then asked for permission to kill her. He again forgave her and replied, "Don't kill her."[19]

His pattern of conduct, shaped by the core value of forgiveness, was a manifestation of the teachings in God's revelation. It is stipulated in the *Qur'an* that it is the Muslims' duty to forgive even when they are angry.[20] The *Qur'an* also clearly states that:

> The recompense for an injury
>
> Is an injury equal thereto
>
> (In degree): but if a person
>
> Forgives and makes reconciliation,
>
> His reward is due
>
> From God: for (God)
>
> Loveth not those who
>
> Do wrong.[21]

It follows from this verse that forgiveness and reconciliation are the correct things to do in a situation of conflict. Moreover, since forgiveness is a value clearly advocated in the *Qur'an*, this means that Islam believes that human beings are capable of living it. Forgiveness is the remedy against the irreversibility of past actions.[22] As a process between two conflicting parties,

---

18 Al-Gazzali, *Ihya Ulum-id-Din*, Book II, p. 271.
19 *Ibid*
20 *Al-Quran*, XLII: 37.
21 Ibid.
22 Geiko Muller-Fahrenholz, "Is Forgiveness in Politics Possible?: 10

forgiveness becomes an act of mutual liberation, the forgiving and the forgiven. It serves to alter social relations so that peace in the future becomes possible.

The five core values of Islam—patience, respect for the humanity of others, sharing, creativity, and forgiveness—identified from both of these incidents in the life of the Prophet, are conducive to peacemaking. But these values are the manifestations of the Divine purpose embedded in the quest of Prophet Muhammad. As a result, there is a need to situate these values within the teleological meaning of the Prophet's existence so that their potentials can be unlocked.

COMPASSION AS A KEY TO THE PROPHETIC PARADIGM

What has been discussed thus far primarily concerns the notion of peace as an absence of direct violence. One of the reasons is that Islam has a clear position on structural violence. The *Qur'an* states:

> And fight them on
>
> Until there is no more
>
> Tumult or oppression
>
> And there prevail
>
> Justice and faith in God
>
> Altogether and everywhere.[23]

Theses," paper presented at the 13th General Conference of the International Peace Research Association, Groningen, The Netherlands, July 3-7, 1990.
23 *Al-Quran*, VIII: 39

It can be argued that Islam as a faith strongly emphasizes the absence of structural violence.[24] In the area of direct violence, it is the concept of jihad that is highly problematic. This concept is generally understood as a holy war waged by Muslims against the unbelievers or enemies of Islam. But contrary to common understanding, jihad is described in the *Qur'an* as an effort or struggle to resist instincts that seek to drive humankind away from belief in God.[25] Classical Muslim scholars such as Ibn Taymiya, for example, argue that jihad is achieved by the heart, the tongue, or the hand. Jihad of the heart, or a struggle against one's own weaknesses or inner evil, is often described as the "greater jihad," whereas the "lesser jihad" is fought against external enemies.[26]

Given Islam's rich tradition, it is important to note that core values conducive to peacemaking can be identified as discussed above. Because the Prophet's practices are used as a paradigm for human actions, it is imperative to discuss the teleological meaning of his existence.

Several verses in the *Qur'an* clearly indicate the Divine Purpose of Prophet Muhammad's existence. He is said to have been sent by God as a "Mercy to those of you who believe."[27] Because God's Mercy is not selective, another verse in *Al-Qur'an* inclusively states that: "We sent thee (Mohammed) not, but/As a Mercy for all creatures."[28]

It is this universal compassion that permeates the existence of

---

24 Johan Galtung, "Religion as a Factor," in Glenn D. Paige (ed.), *Buddhism and Leadership for Peace* (Honolulu: Dae Won Sa, Temple of Hawaii, 1984), figs. 4 and 5, pp. 67-68.
25 *Al-Quran*, II: 218, IV: 95-96, IX: 19.
26 See Chapter II: The Nonviolent Crescent" in this volume
27 *Al-Quran*, IX: 61.
28 *Al-Quran*, XXI: 107.

the Prophet. His actions and practices emerge from such existence and the values identified above are therefore its manifestations. In addition, this compassion that informs the Prophetic paradigm also helps unlock the potentials of the five core values.

From compassion, the will to be patient flows. Compassion also makes it easier to respect other's humanity which will, in turn, be conducive to sharing. Without compassion, cessation of hatred informed by the negative memory of the past will be difficult and therefore forgiveness will become next to impossible. Creativity as a value is more problematic. Creativity in the use of violence is prevalent, as evidenced by the advancement of military technology. Compassion can harness creativity to direct it in ways conducive to peace.

Using the Prophet's practices as a paradigm, Islam offers a set of interrelated core values conducive to nonviolent peacemaking. The idea of compassion that governs the universe serves as a powerful guide to unlock the full power of these values and to help human beings realize their potentials as peacemakers.

Chapter IV

The Islamic Tunes of Gandhi's Ahimsa

The image of a close relationship between Islam and the sword is quite prevalent. This image is not only created out of innocence but also from fear and ignorance. During the later part of the nineteenth century, for example, the Revd Dr C.G. Pfander, a missionary, who was active among Indian Muslims, wrote: "If we study the behaviour of Muhammad's followers, we notice that they thought it was not necessary for them to follow a religious and moral code. God demanded from them only one thing: that they should fight for God with swords, arrows, daggers, and sabres to continue to kill."[1]

This kind of century-old missionary writing contributes to the current image of Islam and the sword, which in turn, is occasionally revitalized by a lack of attention to Islamic contribution to peace and nonviolence.

---

1 Quoted in Hazrat Mirza Tahir Ahmad, *Murder in the Name of Allah,* Syed Barakat Ahmad (trans. from Urdu) (Cambridge: Lutterworth press, 1989), p. 14. Written by a controversial Muslim spiritual leader, this book is an interesting critique of Muslims who try to justify the use of violence by using their religion.

In a textbook on nonviolence, the editor wisely begins with a chapter on its origins. While the origins of nonviolence in Eastern philosophy and religion (Jainism, Taoism, and Hinduism) as well as Occidental traditions, namely Christianity and Judaism, are well covered, Islam as an origin of nonviolence is conspicuously absent.[2]

But perhaps the most disturbing disregard for facts about Islam and nonviolence appears in another book with the title *The Handbook of Nonviolence*. The writer divides the book into two parts. Aldous Huxley's *Encyclopedia of Pacifism*, which originally appeared in 1937, is published as the first part. The second is a selection of significant topics in the field of nonviolence arranged alphabetically. Under the topic "Gandhi, Mohandas K.," the author writes: "In 1948 Gandhi was assassinated by a Moslem who saw the nonviolence campaign as a step towards the subjugation of Moslems by Hindus."[3] Anyone who is familiar with modern Indian history or Gandhi's life should be extremely shocked for they must know well that Gandhi was in fact assassinated by a Hindu, not a Muslim, and the reason given in *The Handbook* is a dangerous fantasy. In an excellent biography of Gandhi, Geoffrey Ashe aptly, though indirectly, states one of the reasons the Mahatma was

---

[2] See Robert L. Holmes (ed.), *Nonviolence in Theory and Practice* (Belmont, California: Wadsworth Publishing Company, 1990), pp. 7-40. However, it is important to point out two facts. First, in the final chapter on "Recent Examples of Nonviolence," the case of Badshah Khan, a nonviolent Muslim leader, is included (pp. 187-191). Second, Islam is not the only religion left out in this edited textbook. The absence of Buddhism as an inspiring origin of nonviolence is perhaps even more difficult to justify given its clear injunction on non-killing.
[3] Robert Seeley, *The Handbook of Nonviolence* (Westport, Conn.: Lawrence Hill & Company; New York: Lakeville Press, 1986), p. 177.

assassinated which is quite opposite to what the author of *The Handbook* has written. He writes: "Pakistan realized that Gandhi had died for his defence of their own people. The Hindu saint was a martyr for the Muslims."[4]

The blunder in Seeley's book is serious for two reasons. First, written as "*The Handbook*" on nonviolence, it effectively reaffirms the image of close approximation between Islam and violence. Second, more importantly, it makes a Muslim responsible for the death of the gentle apostle of nonviolence. A critique of the image of Islam and violence, Islamic theoretical contribution to nonviolence, as well as difficulties in strengthening the linkage between the two has been examined elsewhere.[5] This chapter then, will seek to concentrate on the second point relating to the significance of Seeley's mistake stated above.

Seeley's mistake should be countered by a more radical approach than merely stating the historical fact on who killed Gandhi. This chapter is an attempt to argue that at the core of Gandhi's nonviolence, traces of Islamic teaching can be identified. Specifically, the concept of Gandhi's Ahimsa will be examined from a Muslim's perspective and congeniality between the concept and the faith outlined. I will begin by providing a set of arguments explaining why this linkage between Islam and Ahimsa exists. Then, the Islamic tunes which seem to be hidden in the concept of Ahimsa will be identified.

---

4 Geoffrey Ashe, *Gandhi* (New York: Stein and Day, 1969), pp. 382-383. See also Newman Rosenthal, The Uncompromising Truth: Mahatma Gandhi 1869-1948 (Australia: Nelson, 1969), pp. 134-136. For a fictionalized version of Gandhi's assassination, see Manohar Malgonkar, *The Men Who Killed Gandhi* (Delhi: Orient Paperback, 1981). Malgonkar claims to receive much information for his fiction from the assassin, Nathuram Godse's, collaborators.
5 See Chapter II and Chapter VII in this volume..

Islam and Gandhi

Gandhi's interest in living religion is well-known. When it comes to religious literature, he was an avid reader. He is known to have read Arnold's *The Light of Asia*. He loved "Sermon on the Mount" and adored *Bhagavadgita* (The Song Celestial). He was very much impressed with the Prophet Muhammad as depicted in Carlyle's *Heroes and Hero Worship* as well as Washington Irving's *Life of Mahomet and His Successors*. But it was his kind mother whose influence on religious matters touched him so very deeply.

As a profoundly religious woman, Putlibai, Gandhi's mother, went to the temple daily, never took a meal before prayer, and frequently undertook fasts. C.F. Andrews observes that Gandhi's mother's influence as a devout and gentle Hindu "perpetually returns to his mind and conscience, making the fragrance of the ancient Hindu text so sweet that nothing else in the world can compare with them."[6] But what is also interesting about Gandhi's mother is the fact that she belonged to a sect which infused Islamic ideas into Hinduism, and thus had strict attitudes to sex, alcohol, and tobacco. Daily prayers and fasts were also significant to her.[7] Given her background and her influence on Gandhi, it is logical to suspect traces of Islamic teachings in his notion of Ahimsa.

Gandhi's feeling towards Islam is one of respect. He certainly considers Islam as "one of the inspired religions, and therefore the Holy Koran as an inspired book and Muhammad as one of the prophets."[8] It is also possible to point to the fact that

---

6 Quoted in K.L. Seshagiri Rao, *Mahatma Gandhi and Comparative Religion* (Delhi Varanasi and Patna: Motilal Banarsidass, 1978), p. 2.
7 Geoffrey Ashe, *Gandhi*, pp. 4-5.
8 Quoted in K.L. Seshagiri Rao, *Mahatma Gandhi and Comparative Religion*, p. 38.

Gandhi's belief in the inseparability between politics and spiritual yearning is influenced by the example of Prophet Muhammad. In fact, C.F. Andrews clearly states in his *Mahatma Gandhi's Ideas:*

Following the example of the Prophet of Islam, Mahatma Gandhi has never for a moment separated the political from the spiritual, or failed to deal directly with the social evil which stood out before his eyes. Thus the Prophet's supreme, practical instinct as a reformer, combined with his intense faith in God as the sole Creater and Director of the Universe, has been a great source of constant strength and support to Mahatma Gandhi himself, in his own struggle.[9]

That Gandhi finds Islam inspiring can also be substantiated by the fact that, as suggested by William L. Shirer, an American historian, he read the *Qur'an* for inspiration.[10]

C.F. Andrews also indicates that Gandhi was deeply inspired by the early days of the Prophet's mission. It was the time when Prophet Muhammad was despised and rejected by his own people because he chose to believe differently from them and preach his belief. He faced every form of humiliation in silence and in this Gandhi found that the teaching of the Prophet of Islam is fully compatible with his principle of Ahimsa.[11]

---

9 Quoted in *ibid*
10 William L. Shirer, *Gandhi: A Memoir* (New York: Simon and Schuster, 1979), p. 73. Shirer, however, indicates that although he followed Gandhi's advice, he did not find much inspiration from his reading. If should also be noted that Shirer's rather unfriendly attitude towards Islam is evident throughout this book. See, for example, pages 73 and 115.
11 See K.L. Seshagiri Rao, *Mahatma Gandhi and Comparative Religion*, p. 39.

Nonviolence and Islamic Imperatives

The compatibility between Islamic teaching and Gandhi's concept of Ahimsa finds one of its most concrete manifestations in the life and struggle of Abdul Gaffar Khan, the Frontier Gandhi. He writes:

There is nothing surprising in a Muslim or a Pathan like me subscribing to the creed of nonviolence. It is not a new creed. It was followed fourteen hundred years ago by the Prophet all the time he was in Mecca, and it has since been followed by all those who wanted to throw off an oppressor's yoke. But we had so far forgotten it and when Gandhi placed it before us, we thought he was sponsoring a novel creed.[12]

Abdul Gaffar Khan's life and struggle is beautifully documented elsewhere[13] and it is beyond the scope of this chapter to carefully examine his understanding of the relationship between Islam and nonviolence. I will therefore turn my attention to Gandhi's perception of Abdul Gaffar Khan's nonviolence which is more relevant to the present discussion. When the "nonviolent soldier of Islam" submitted his letter of resignation in 1940 from the Congress Working Committee because of its restriction on the use of nonviolence to the fight for India's freedom against constituted authority, Gandhi tended to support his decision. In fact, he pointed out that Ghaffar Khan's faith dictated his decision. For him, nonviolence is not merely intellectual conviction but "intuitive faith." This is possible because Abdul Ghaffar Khan "derives his Ahimsa from the *Holy Quran*. He is a devout Musalman. During his stay with me [Gandhi] for over a year I never saw him miss his namaz (prayers) or his Ramzan fast except when he was ill."[14]

---

12 Quoted in Eknath Easwaran, *A Man to Match His Mountains: Badshah Khan, Nonviolent Soldiers of Islam* (Petluma, California: Niligiri Press, 1984), p. 103.
13 *Ibid.*
14 M.K. Gandhi, *Nonviolence in Peace and War* (Ahmedabad: Navaji-

According to Gandhi, Abdul Ghaffar Khan's strength in his adherence to Ahimsa is due to his strong personal faith in Islam. I am aware of the significance of the inner and personal dimension of inclination towards nonviolence. But as a social scientist, I would rather not confine my framework of analysis to only the strength or weakness of the individual involved. Besides, it seems inadequate to explain the fact that Abdul Gaffar Khan was not the only Muslim who participated in Gandhi's nonviolent struggle. As a matter of fact, Dr. Sayyed Mahmud, a leading Muslim and a general secretary of the Congress, said that although many Muslims held back their support for Gandhi and the Congress because their leaders feared Hindu domination, twelve thousand Muslims were jailed during the nonviolent campaign. In addition, five hundred Muslims had been killed since Gandhi started his march to the sea in 1930.[15]

Two other possible explanations can still be offered. First, Islam is inherently conductive to nonviolence and therefore some Muslims will be naturally inclined towards Ahimsa. However, as mentioned above, this mode of explanation had already been tried elsewhere.[16] Second, within Gandhi's concept of Ahimsa, there are traces of Islamic teachings and therefore it is possible for those Muslims to follow Gandhi in his struggle along the path of Ahimsa. It is this second formulation to which I will now turn.

---

van Publishing House, 1948), Vol. I, p. 298.
15 William Shirer, *Gandhi: A Memoir*, p. 156.
16 See note 5 above.

Gandhi's Ahimsa and the Islamic Tunes Within

Gandhi's Ahimsa is a rich and complex concept. Joan Bondurant, for example, suggests that the term expresses an ancient Hindu, Jain, and Buddhist ethical precept. Accepting the fact that the wording is negative, she contends that in Hindu and Buddhist traditions, it implies much more which remains unexpressed. It is basically an action based upon refusal to do harm.[17]

But with careful consideration, the term Ahimsa emerges on its own as a positive concept. Because the word himsa means to injure, kill, or destroy, it is already a negative concept. Apply the word to human beings and/or societies, then it implies a reduction, a cessation, or a curtailment of their existence or potentialities. Consequently, when the prefix "a" is used in front of the term himsa, it turns into a double negative and therefore a positive concept.

There has been much discussion on the positive characteristics of Ahimsa.[18] Gandhi himself spent much of his time answering queries about what is and is not nonviolence or Ahimsa. In 1946 he wrote: "At every step he (man) has to use his discrimination as to what is Ahimsa and what is himsa."[19] Perhaps, a different question about the concept should serve the discussion better.

In its most concrete form, Ahimsa is a renunciation of killing with the possibility of dying. It is a radical shift of death of

---

17 Joan v. Bondurant, *The Conquest of Violence: The Gandhian Philosophy of Conflict* (Berkeley and Los Angeles: University of California Press, 1967), p. 23.
18 See, for example, M.V. Naidu's discussion of the concept by linking it to *prema* (love) in his "The Gandhian Vision of the Ideal Political Society," *Peace Research*, Vol. 19 No. 3 (September 1987), pp. 79-80.
19 M.K. Gandhi, *Nonviolence in Peace and War*, Vol. II, p. 69.

one's adversary to one's own. It is a most difficult concept because in its action-oriented nature, it does not merely ask the votary of nonviolence to stop killing others, but to prepare to die. Gandhi suggests that Satyagraha or Truth Force which basically means the power of Truth manifested through nonviolence, is in fact "the art of living and dying." He writes:

> The art of dying follows as a corollary from the art of living. Death must come to all. A man may die of a lightning stroke, or as a result of heart failure, or failure of respiration. But that is not the death that a Satyagrahi can wish for or pray for himself. The art of dying for a Satyagrahi consists in facing death cheerfully in the performance of one's duty.[20]

The last sentence deserves careful consideration. The practitioner of Ahimsa must perform his/her duty. He/she must do something for the sake of Truth. Practitioners of Ahimsa seek to conquer evil by the Force of Truth. Therefore Gandhi wrote: "Ahimsa is not the way of the timid or the cowardly. It is the way of the brave ready to face death. He who perishes sword in hand is no doubt brave, but he who faces death without raising his little finger and without flinching is braver."[21] Gandhi even develops a category of action which he terms "almost nonviolence." For example, he would call women who, in defence of their honour, used their nail, teeth or a dagger as acting almost nonviolently.[22] The point is the issue of harming or not harming the one who is trying to dishonour the women is less relevant than the issue of action and inaction. Echoing Gene Sharp's dictum, it is action which counts in the field of nonviolence.

---

20 *Ibid.*, p. 63.
21 M.K. Gandhi, *Nonviolence in Peace and War*, Vol. I, p. 76.
22 M.K. Gandhi, *My Nonviolence* (Ahmedabad: Navajivan Publishing House, 1960), p. 145.

Nonviolence and Islamic Imperatives

Muslims can easily recognize a definite trace of Islam from all this. Regarding death, they should be willing to die in the Way of God. Death for the Muslims is a return to Allah. *Al-Quran* says: "To God we belong, and to Him is our return."[23] An inclination towards action is also easily recognizable for the Muslims. *Al-Qur'an* repeatedly instructs the Muslims to act against "tumult and oppression." It says:

> And fight them on
>
> Until there is no more
>
> Tumult or oppression,
>
> And there prevail
>
> Justice and faith in God
>
> Altogether and everywhere.[24]

If fighting is considered an essence of Ahimsa, then it is not unfamiliar for the Muslims. There are then two questions left at this point, namely the purpose of fighting and its methods.

For the Muslims, the purpose of fighting is also clear. They fight for the sake of God. *Al-Qur'an* says:

> Fight in the cause of God
>
> Those who fight you
>
> But do not transgress limits;
>
> For God loveth no transgressors.[25]

The dialectical relationship of Truth and nonviolence in terms of ends and means notwithstanding, in the final analysis of

---

23 *Al-Qur'an*, II: 156. Here I am using *The Glorious Qur'an*, translated by A. Yusuf Ali (US.: Muslim Student's Association, 1977).
24 *Al-Qur'an*, VIII: 39.
25 *Al-Qur'an.*, II: 190.

Gandhi's Ahimsa, Truth is the goal.[26] For Gandhi, Satya is the greatest Truth which is the unity of all life. His metaphysical claim is "Truth is God" and following this, he would be able to "...see God face to face as it were. I feel him pervade every fibre of my being."[27] If Truth exists within every life, then the greatest good of all life cannot be pursued by ways which would lead to the destruction of life itself. Therefore, Ahimsa is the only way to pursue Truth because himsa or violence would offend the greatest Truth which is the unity and sacredness of all life.

Some scholars may argue that in discussing Satya, Gandhi merely espoused a Hindu concept and Hinduism is a compilation of different systems of philosophies and ethics ranging from atheism to polytheism and monotheism. As a result, it is quite different from the theological, anthropomorphic, and personalized God in other religions.[28] I would argue that a Muslim can still recognize his/her God from Gandhi's notion for two reasons. First, if Hinduism is that multi-dimensional, then it must have something for everyone including the Muslims. Second, the nature of God in Islam has His non-personal attributes. In fact, the Divine Name Allah is the synthesis of all truth. God has many names and each of the Names of the Divine Essence comprises in Itself the totality of Names and does not merely denote a particular Divine Aspect. Al-Haqq or Truth is one such Name.[29] Moreover, there is a specific Qur'anic injunction

---

26 M.K. Gandhi, *Nonviolence in Peace and War*, Vol. I, p. 414..
27 *Ibid.*, Vol. II, p. 104. Here he writes: "Ahimsa is not the goal. Truth is the goal. But we have no means of realizing truth in human relationships except through the practice of *Ahimsa*."
28 M.V. Naidu, "The Gandhian Vision of the Ideal Political Society," p. 74.
29 Martin Lings, *What is Sufism?* (Berkeley and Los Angeles: Univer-

which would support the notion of Ahimsa in harming no other life. *Al-Quran* says: "Whithersoever ye turn, there is the Presence of God."[30] If this is the case, then it is not possible for a Muslim to harm other living things without at the same time offending God which is Truth.

Concerning methods of fighting, Gandhi's Ahimsa is more complex than a refrain from using physical violence. In fact, Gandhi writes:

> ...My nonviolence fully accommodated violence offered by those who did not feel nonviolence and who had in their keeping the honour of their womenfolk and little children. Nonviolence is not a cover for cowardice, but it is the supreme virtue of the brave...Translation from swordsmanship to nonviolence is possible and, at times, even an easy stage. Nonviolence, therefore, presupposes ability to strike.[31]

A Muslim can easily identify traces of Islam in this kind of statement. What is important for a Muslim is the fact Islam is all-pervasive and every aspect of life is included within the religious sphere. In other words, moral quality exists in every human action, great or small.

In addition, Gandhi also outlined a set of conditions necessary for the successful use of nonviolence in the service of Truth. First, the person should not have any hatred in his/her heart against his/her opponent. Second, the issue must be true and substantial. Third, he or she must be prepared to suffer till the end. Fourth, the root of such action lies in prayer for the sake of god's protection.[32]

---

sity of California Press, 1977), p. 64.
30 *Al-Qur'an*, II: 115.
31 M.K. Gandhi, *Nonviolence in Peace and War*, Vol. I, pp. 59-60.
32 *Ibid.*, Vol. II, pp. 61-62.

Any Muslim would find the last three conditions rather easy to understand. Fighting for the sake of Truth is essential for the faith. The issue must be morally justified. The Prophet once said: "Do for this world as if thou were to live a thousand years and for the next as if thou were to die tomorrow."[33] Consequently, suffering for the sake of God is regarded with respect. Moreover, the Muslims are used to the practice of suffering in their daily life. The Muslims would be very much at home with fasting, a form of nonviolent action, because it is considered one of the Islamic pillars. Prayers is also a daily activity among the Muslims. Islamic prayers perform two basic functions, bringing the Muslims face to face with God and to review his/her life as a form of meditative self-examination. With profound conviction, prayers will give them strength to live or die for the sake of Truth.

What I have attempted in this chapter is not to show the extent to which Islamic teachings influenced Gandhi's notion of Ahimsa. I merely argue that possibility for such an influence does exist. If such is the case, the fact that Gandhi's Ahimsa appeals to some Muslims can be explained by not using Islam or the individual Muslim as factor. Instead, I suggest that the Islamic tunes within Gandhi's Ahimsa which some Muslims are able to identify can be used as an explanatory factor.

Conclusion: Prospects for Nonviolent Muslims

Many years ago, Kenneth Boulding tried to apprehend Gandhi's failure. His main thesis is that nonviolence is only effective when aligned with truth. But truth in the modern world is so complex that it can no longer by perceived by commonsense or by mystical insights. Thus, when truth is

---

33 Quoted in Martin Lings, *What is Sufism?*, p. 34.

rejected and illusion clouds judgement, nonviolence will consequently be rejected.[34] If Boulding is correct in his diagnosis of the current situation, then the Muslims are in a better position to appreciate Ahimsa, because, for them, struggle for "Truth" has never been a problem. Their struggles, if they were to attain religious significance, need to be those in the service of God. For them, one of Allah's attributes is Haqq (Truth). Therefore, Gandhi's Ahimsa due to its inseparability from Truth (Satya) should be quite appealing to the Muslims.

---

34 Kenneth E. Boulding, "Why did Gandhi Fail?," in G. Ramachandran and T.K. Mahadevan (eds.), *Gandhi: His Relevance for Our Time* (Berkeley: World Without War Council, 1971), pp. 129-134.

Chapter V

Muslim Communal Nonviolent Actions: Minority Coexistence in A Non-Muslim Society

One of the most memorable scenes of coexistence between Muslims and non-Muslims I have ever witnessed took place on a Friday afternoon before a *jumaat* prayer near a local mosque in central Bangkok, Thailand. The scene was typical: Muslims from nearby workplaces arrived for the congregation. The mosque, surrounded by both Muslim and non-Muslim communities, was in an alley reachable only on foot. Most come before *Qutbah* (Friday sermon) because in addition to being a place of worship, a mosque is also a place where friends meet, people talk, messages are shared and *halal* food is consumed. Finding a place for Muslim food in Bangkok is not easy because Muslims, though the largest minority in Thai society, are only 7 percent of a country of some 60 million people.[1]

---

1 Even the figure of Muslim population in Thai society is not unproblematic. See my brief discussion of the politics of contending figures of Muslims in Thailand in Chaiwat Satha-Anand, "Bangkok Muslims and the Tourist Trade," in Mohamed Ariff (ed.), *The Muslim Private Sector in Southeast Asia* (Singapore: Institute of Southeast Asian Stu-

On that day, I and several Muslims were having our lunch in front of a small stall in the open basement of a traditional Thai house. The space was small and so crowded with customers that it was difficult to walk through. Suddenly we heard a loud voice: "Here comes the pork!" And the crowded customers having their fried rice or Indian-styled chicken rice parted as if touched by magic. Silently, and as quickly as she could, an elderly Chinese woman carrying a large bowl filled with a pork dish walked through the throngs of Muslims waiting for their Friday prayers. The Chinese woman tried her best to stay clear from the men around her in that narrow pathway while the Muslims tried their utmost to make themselves as small as they could to avoid contact with the prohibited substance. What is remarkable about this scene is the fact that the warning voices echoed from here and there with smiling faces, that the Chinese woman ambled almost apologetically, that the Muslims expressed no anger, and that this scene of everyday coexistence must have been a common one.

As a matter of fact, in India, where Hindu-Muslim conflicts have flared dangerously in recent years, Ashis Nandy maintained that for every riot reported, there are also "instances of bravery shown by persons who protect their neighbors at immense risks to their own lives and that of their families."[2] Even at the time of the bitter partition of the subcontinent, which saw the deaths of hundreds of thousands of people, both Hindu and Muslims, there were stories of someone from the other communities who helped families of the "others."[3] Such coexistence persists, since of the 2,800 Indian communities

---

dies, 1991), pp. 96-97.
2 Ashis Nandy, "The Twilight of Certitudes: Secularism, Hindu Nationalism, and Other Masks of Deculturation," *Alternatives*, 22 (1997), p. 160.
3 *Ibid.*, p. 160.

identified as predominantly Hindu or Muslim in the 1990s, only about 350 were exclusively one or the other. In addition, some 600 such communities also live with multiculturalism within.[4]

Muslim Minority's Nonviolent Action: A Broad Conceptual Guideline

In attempting to understand a Muslim minority's engagement with conflict in a largely non-Muslim setting, I will pose and attempt to answer three basic questions: First, what is the primary purpose of engaging in such conflicts? Second, what is the political context of the majority-minority relationship? Third, what kind of action would allow Muslims minorities to engage in such conflicts meaningfully, constructively, and effectively?

If it is the life of a Muslim minority as a collective identity that is being threatened by the "malady of modernity," then the purpose of engaging in conflict is primarily to defend its community as opposed to fighting to unseat a tyranny. Thailand is a "strong democratic society," judging from the people's rights institutionalized in the constitution of 1997, complete with independent monitoring agencies, competitive electoral politics, and a highly visible civil society[5]. Conflict in such a context would naturally be different from conflict in an authoritarian polity. So the range of potential nonviolent

---

4 See Kumar Suresh Singh, *People of India: An Introduction* (New Delhi: Anthropological Survey of India, 1992), Vol. I, as quoted in Nandy, "The Twilight of Certitudes," fn. 13, p. 174.

5 Since then there have been two coup d'etats, in September 2006 and then again in May 2014. Thailand in 2016 is under a military rule with the coup leader serving as the prime minister who promises that the country would have an election by the end of 2017 or early 2018.

protest for aggrieved parties in Thailand is broad. Generally speaking, nonviolent action may involve "acts of omission," whereby people refuse to perform their expected functions, or "acts of commission," whereby they engage in unexpected or proscribed activities. Nonviolent protests to defend Muslim minorities' way of life in a democracy seem to take the forms of "nonviolent protest and persuasion," mainly symbolic actions of peaceful opposition.

Defending Muslim Communities from Drugs, Pathological Development, and Greed in Fishery

1. Fighting against drugs

One of the most pressing problems facing Thai society is drugs, primarily heroin and amphetamines. According to the United Nations, illegal businesses worldwide generate an annual income of around $ 600 billion, two-thirds of which is from drug trafficking. In Thailand, profits from drug trafficking were estimated at around 21 percent of world total and twice the country's earnings from exports in 1994. The U.S. Bureau of National Narcotic Matter estimated that the production of opium in Southeast Asia accounted for 75 percent of world production in 1993, most of it originated from the Golden Triangle bordering Thailand, Laos and Burma. Prices of heroin at sources of the time were between $ 2,400-3,400 per kg. (using then exchange rate of US$1=45 Thai Bath). But when sold in the US, prices jump to $57,000-122,000 per kg. In 1994-1995, it was estimated that there were more than 214,000 heroin addicts while there were 257,965 amphetamine addicts in 1993. The cost of production of amphetamine is roughly seven to eleven cents per pill, but each could fetch around two dollars in United State market.⁶ The drug business survives and, in fact, thrives because it is protected by dark influences in Thai society, most likely involving the collaboration of some high-ranking politicians and police officers.⁷ It is a small wonder that drugs have become such a gigantic problem in Thai society.

It is remarkable when small communities decide to fight back. For a long time, residents of a community in the outskirt of Bangkok lived in fear of powerful drug gangs who traded openly. The 5.2-acre town is called "Mitraparb" (friendship) community but is better known among residents as "Apache Village." It has a population of 800, mostly Muslims who work in factories and small-scale commercial business. Theft and petty crime were rampant as drug addiction spread among community members. Reliance on the compromised local police proved futile. In October 1997, members of the community decided that "enough is enough" and called a town meeting to mobilize a response to the problem. They decided to set up a round-the-clock security service, with villagers taking turns on foot patrol. The aroused locals were able to apprehend seventeen buyers on the very first night. From October 1997 to June 1998, sixty-four users and/or dealers were apprehended. A community leader reported that most of the pushers were people from outside the community. When they were checked by the community security team, their names and ID card numbers were recorded. All were told that they would be handed to the police if they came back. As a

---

6 All these figures are from Pasuk Phongpaichit, Sungsidh Piriyarangsan and Nualnoi Treerat, *Guns, Girls, Gambling, Ganja: Thailand's Illegal Economy and Public Policy* (Chiang Mai: Silkworm Books, 1998), pp. 86-111.
7 It is possible to find such collaborations elsewhere in the region. See for example, Alfred W. McCoy, *The Politics of Heroin in Southeast Asia* (New York: Harper and Row, 1972).

result of their action, the crime rate has dropped sharply. Women and children can walk the streets without fear again.[8]

Seeing its success, the Bangkok Metropolitan Administration has chosen this Muslim community to lead a pilot project in a move to declare fifty communities drug-free zones. Members of Mitraparb community were asked to advise others on possible courses of action. This is a case of an ordinary urban village being threatened by a drug problem that robbed the villagers of their sense of safety that, in turn, altered the situation by empowering themselves. This Muslim community is admired by both the Thai authorities and other non-Muslim communities that also seek to root out the drug peddlers by such means of empowerment.

2. Fighting Against Pathological Development

Bangkok, a city of more than 7 million people, has its share of urban problems, with traffic congestion near the top of the list. The diagnosis of this problem is simple: too many cars on too few roads. According to the mayor of Bangkok, there are more than 4 million cars in Bangkok, while there are only 2,812 km. of roads of all type.[9] The mainstream solution is to build more roads.[10] The first National Economic Development Plan, formulated some four decades ago, included proposals to modernize the country's infrastructure; most canals in the city, which had once served as transportation channels and a natural drainage system, were filled with earth to build roads. Recently,

---

8 Ampa Santimetaneedol, "Villagers find courage to drive out drug dealers," *Bangkok Post*, June 8, 1998.

9 *Situation in Thai Society, 1997: A Summary* (Bangkok: Thai Development Support Committee, February 1998), p. 60. (In Thai)

10 See a critical view of mainstream development in Saneh Chamarik, *Development and Democracy: A Cultural Perspective* (Bangkok: Local Development Institute, 1993).

numerous megaprojects such as the sky train and a subway system have sprung up in Bangkok as if the city could grow indefinitely. The expressway project is one such megaproject the government planned and carried out in order to alleviate traffic problems.

But to build such an extensive highway at a time when the city is bursting at the seams is to risk a number of crucial problems. For example, appropriation of land already owned by Bangkok residents has become a costly endeavor on the part of the expressway builder and the administration. There are landowners who accept compensation, normally below market prices, without any fight. There are those, however, who do not yield so easily and have taken their cases to court. One of the most famous and instructive examples is the fight of the Ban Krua community.

Some might think of Ban Krua as one of Bangkok's 843 slums. With more than 1.1 million inhabitants, this area includes 14.6 percent of Bangkok's population.[11] So when it was suggested that one of the exits of the second stage expressway has to cut through Ban Krua, the choice seems obvious: a slum vs. a gleaming new road to ease congestion for Bangkok's growing and thriving middle class. The people of Ban Krua had other ideas, however. They have argued that they do not want to obstruct the expressway project; they simply do not want to be forced from their homes for a roadway that they contend will aggravate rather than alleviate the city's traffic congestion. The fight of Ban Krua community has been going on for more than thirteen years, with that expressway exit yet to materialize on the backs of that poor community.

---

11 These figures are those of National Housing Authority. See *Situation of Thai Society 1997: A Summary*, p. 27. (In Thai)

Why have they fought so hard for their community? Commenting on a columnist's remark that there are others whose land and houses were dug up more than once under the cruel claws of these megaprojects, a Ban Krua community leader observed, "What I feel for and will not be able to find elsewhere is much more than houses. It is the air of the community that everyone knows everyone. We can greet anyone from one house to the next everyday. If we are driven away from here, this atmosphere will be gone."[12] This strong communal sense is rooted in long-standing Cambodian Muslim identity of the area, which was founded some two hundred years ago.[13] In a great battle between the Burmese and the Siamese in the reign of King Rama I (1782-1809), known as "the nine-army battle", the Cham (Cambodian Muslims) volunteered to fight on the side of the King. When the Burmese were defeated, in an act of appreciation, King Rama I graciously granted a piece of land to be the home of the community of these brave Cambodian Muslims who fought and died for Siam and the King. Ban Krua residents also claim that as a Muslim community, they have built both a mosque and a cemetery that cannot be touched or removed because they are *waqf* (Islamic endowment of property to be held in trust and used for a religious purpose). Even if the expressway exit were to avoid both sacred grounds, a mosque without any community to sustain it with lives, prayers, and spirituality would not mean much.

The Ban Krua community has fought the modern project using all types of nonviolent methods. Sometimes they sent

---

12 Seksan Prasertkul, "Ban Krua Ban Krai," *Manager's Daily*, April 25, 1994. (In Thai)

13 Muslims in Thai society are not monolithic. There are, in fact, at least six lineages of Muslims in the country: Chinese, Persian, Indian/Pakistani, Arab, Cambodian and Malay Muslims. See Chaiwat Satha-Anand, "Bangkok Muslims and the Tourist Trade," pp. 96-97.

letters asking for help from the authorities; they also worked with the opposition to pressure the then governments. Internally, they organized themselves to protect their community with guards and patrol teams because, as a slum, the community is susceptible to arsons. In fact, there have been attempts to set fire to houses in Ban Krua, but they were put out by the residents themselves. Everyone helps. Even children in the community are trained to identify any suspicious occurrence or person. They have organized cultural tours of their community, famous for its production of refined silk and indigenous Islamic cuisine. These nonviolent tactics have proved effective politically and have won wide admiration among non-Muslim segments of Bangkok.

But the leaders of the protest have not shied away from street actions, either. In April 1994, the community descended on the government house, demanding to see the prime minister. They have used all kinds of symbolic nonviolent actions to convey the message that they are serious about their fight and that they are willing to sacrifice whatever it takes to fight for their rights and for what is right. For example, they called for a press conference and digging the grave in the community cemetery to show the public that they were willing to lay down their lives in this fight. Prayers were offered before the demonstration. People put on their "Muslim" garb, including turbans, kapiyah (head covers for men) or hijab (head covers for women). Some carried coffins covered with velvet cloth adorned with words from the holy *Qur'an* Surah II (Al-Bakara), Verse 156: "To Allah we belong, and to Him is our return." Once they arrived in front of the government house, they set up their community there. Compulsory prayers, uttered five times a day, were offered for everyone to see. They also sent protest letters to several Muslim countries around the world.[14]

14 See account of this particular protest in *Managers'Daily*, April 22, 1994. (In Thai)

After three days, the prime minister came out to meet the Muslims of Ban Krua, who greeted him kindly and with delight. Before he left them, they all made supplications (*du'a*) asking Allah Almighty to bless him with wisdom to distinguish right from wrong.[15] All the leading newspaper columnists agreed on the exemplary quality of Ban Krua Muslims' protests. They wrote that the nonviolent struggle of Ban Krua Muslims is a "model" for Thai civil society, "a fight of courageous people's warrior worthy of becoming future lesson," "an example for to contemplate changes in Thai society."[16]

The Ban Krua Muslims have been fighting to defend their community from a kind of modernization that sacrifices the values of tradition, spirit, and community for the sake of dubious material gains. The most salient quality of their nonviolent struggle is their success in using Islamic religious practices and symbols to assert their identity as a Muslim community with a glorious history of serving Thai society valiantly in the past. A researcher who did her thesis on the protest of Ban Krua community concludes that conditions of their success is based on the leadership's faith in religion and belief that communal responsibility of the leaders is "God's obligation." A community leader told the researcher that, "We are limited in every way. Without God's guidance, would we be able to do this? To move forward in fighting is to walk with God."[17]

---

15 Kaewsan Atipothi, "Mob 'Ban Krua': Flash of Democracy in front of the Government House?," *Managers' Daily*, May 3, 1994. (In Thai)
16 *Managers'Daily*, April 25, 1994; April 22, 1994; and May 3, 1994. (In Thai)
17 Chalida Tajaroensuk, Protesting Process of Ban-Krua Community on 2nd Stage Expressway System Project (Collector-Distributor Road), Master's Degree Thesis, Faculty of Social Development, National Institute of Development Administration (NIDA), 1996, p. 86 (In Thai). This thesis also underscores the use of nonviolent actions by the Ban-Krua community.

3. Fighting Against Greed in Fishery

Thailand has a 2,600-km coastline that extends 1,700-km in the south. In 1990, there were 47,000 households headed by fishermen; the livelihood of at least half a million people depends solely on the ocean, and 74 percent of these people are in southern Thailand. There are two kinds of fishermen: Small and large commercial types. The small operators with small boats or no boat at all number approximately 30,000 households in the south, constitute some 85 percent of the population of small fishermen in the country, and cannot fish beyond 3 km offshore because of the big commercial fishing trawlers, which often invade that 3-km zone and thus infringe on the livelihood of the small operators. If small fishermen choose to invest more in their fishing instruments, they often end up with lots of debts. At present, they earn $526-$927 a year while their expenses amount to approximately $927 a year.[18]

In recent years, as seafood has become more and more commercially viable, big trawlers try to catch more fish by moving closer to the shore with no seasonal surcease. To secure their livelihood against big business' code of greed, southern fishermen from four provinces around Phangnga Bay want the government to expand the coastal zone where trawling is not allowed. They want to extend the protected zone from the existing 673 sq. km to 2,010 sq. km to permit the rehabilitation of fish stocks. On June 24, 1998, Muslim fishermen from the area decided to call on the director-general of Fishery Department. A fisherman said to his friends, "We all suffer the

---

18 Lessons of Non-Government Organizations on Resources and Environment in the South, A seminar document prepared for "Thai Non-Government Organizations: Looking Back and Ahead: A Seminar to commemorate the first decade of Non-Government Organization Coordinating Committee," January 28–29, 1997, pp. 1-2.

effects of those big trawlers taking away our resources. We should tell as many people as possible to come and listen to what the government has to say. We don't have any physical force, but if we come in large numbers, we can at least muster some power."[19]

In preparing for the confrontation, a question was asked about measures that could be used to pressure "the other." A Muslim elder of the fishing community answered, "No matter what, don't use violence. It's no good for anybody. We should try our best and aim for peaceful talks." Muslim fishermen around the Phangnga Bay area were all enthusiastic about the initiative. They organized themselves by soliciting voluntary contributions to fund the cost of their nonviolent actions. They also prepared their own food to take along with them. Finally, 3,000 small-scale fishermen went to Krabi City Hall. But they did not enter into a trilateral discussion with government officials and the commercial trawler operators because they were dissatisfied with the number of their representatives allowed to attend the negotiation. Having boycotted the negotiation, Muslim fishermen decided to stage a nonviolent sit-in cum blockade.[20] Protesters made a barricade to stop officials and the commercial trawler operators from entering and leaving City Hall so that they would have to listen to their side of argument.

The way in which they organize their nonviolent actions is culturally creative. For example, Muslim women were assigned to guard the gate of City. A Muslim woman in her hijab[21] told

---

19 Supara Janchitfah, "Charting their own course," *Bangkok Post* (Outlook Section), July 16, 1998.
20 For 198 methods of nonviolent action, see Gene Sharp, *The Politics of Nonviolent Action (Part Two): The Methods of Nonviolent Action* (Boston: Porter Sargent, 1973).
21 For the politics of wearing hijab in Thai society see Chaiwat Satha-

a reporter that women are gentle, "so we should keep vigil at the gate." Another pointed out, "Muslim women don't only have to live behind the veil and pray five times a day. We can and must exercise our rights. That is what our Imam told us." The barricade sparked a war of words as tensions rose. People were attacked with sticks and stones until both group leaders were able to calm their friends down and separate the contending parties. Finally the governor agreed to talk with the fishermen. An agreement was reached that a committee would be formed in the following four months to study the proposed enlarged protected zone. The fishermen (and women) then prayed to Allah to express their gratitude that their efforts were met with moderate success. A fisherman said, "At least the officials listened to us and left the door of opportunity open for further study." When asked what would happen if the fishermen's demands remained unsatisfied in four months, the fisherman answered, "I believe more of us will go there again."[22]

For a group of 3,000 fishermen with little experience in communal nonviolent action, the degree to which they were able to adjust their tactics in accordance with changing circumstances was quite impressive. Another remarkable feature of the Muslim fishermen's struggle was the fact that they decided early on to conduct their protest nonviolently.

A distinguished Thai journalist wrote that the Muslim fishermen tried everything. When told to get organized, they did. When told to consult the law, they found that the 3-km

---

Anand, "Hijab and Moments of Legitimation: Islamic Resurgence in Thai Society," in Charles F. Keyes, Laurel Kendall and Helen Hardacre (eds.), *Asian Visions of Authority: Religion and the Modern States of East and Southeast Asia*. (Honolulu: University of Hawaii Press, 1994), pp. 279-300.
22 Supara Janchitfah, "Charting Their Own Course."

no-entry law against trawlers was on their side. When told to complain to government officials, moving up the bureaucratic ladder from the marine police up to the head of government, they did that, too. Finally, they took to the streets, which she claims is "the last resort for the poor to air their grievances." Again, they were told to start a dialogue, with every side involved. They did that and organized themselves into a united, regional network. Yet the authorities refuse to act because, the journalist argues, there is a lack of legal enforcement.[23]

Nevertheless, the quality of the fishermen's participation in this conflict is quite instructive. Through their communal actions, they become stronger. They also learned that there is power in numbers.[24] To ensure a large number of participants, efficient organization and creative methods were necessary. The Muslim fishermen were able to get themselves organized through tapping their strength as a Muslim community in their creative and highly adaptive nonviolent struggle against greed.

Muslim Communal Nonviolent Actions: Some Common Features?

These three cases of Muslim communal nonviolent actions show some interesting similarities and contrasts. First, each case is different as regards the extent of preparation, experience, and time involved. The Ban Krua Muslims were the most experienced, given their longstanding grievances. On the

---

23 Sanitsuda Ekachai, "Reform before it is too late," *Bangkok Post* (Commentary), September 24, 1998.

24 But number alone may not be enough. Compare also Gustavo Gutierrez, *The Power of the Poor in History*, Robert R. Barr (trans.) (Quezon City, Philippines: Claretian Publications, 1985).

other hand, the fishermen of Phangnga seemed to move into communal nonviolent action without much experience. The "Mitraparb" urban village showed the most patience before coalescing into militant action to fight the drug dealers.

The fishermen's three days of confrontation and four months of waiting for the result was the shortest episode, while the decade-long struggle of the Ban Krua community is the longest. The "Mitraparb" village's eight-month struggle falls in between.

Second, the social background of each community is different. Ban Krua and "Mitraparb" Muslims are quite similar because both communities are urban, with a good representation of small businesspeople and factory workers. On the other hand, the fishermen of the Southern Sea are rural people. In terms of educational background, the Ban Krua Muslims are perhaps the best educated.

Third, the relationship between the communities and state agencies in general is different in each case. While the "Mitraparb" community is on very good terms with the authorities, both the Ban Krua Muslims and the fishermen are not. This is because the causes they are fighting against are different.

Fourth, the "Mitraparb" community's fight against drug pushers dovetailed with official state policy, whereas the struggles against the highway exit and the big fishermen pitted poor people against entrenched interests defended by the government.

Fifth, the degree to which each community is committed to nonviolent action differs. It seems that the fishermen were most vocal about their commitment to nonviolence, while the "Mitraparb" community most inclined to resort to force if necessary. As a matter of fact, one of their banners read: "We will not forgive the damned drug pushers."²⁵ The Ban Krua community is distinctive in its varied uses of nonviolent techniques. Most of the methods Ban Krua people fell under the category of symbolic nonviolent protest.

On the other hand, there are five basic similarities in the protests that were significant in helping these minority Muslim communities win the admiration of the surrounding non-Muslim majority.

1. Just Cause

Each struggle was widely perceived as a just cause. The "Mitraparb" crusade against drug pushers struck a chord among both Muslims and non-Muslim afflicted by that plague. Their community has been fighting against drug problems. The Ban Krua community has been fighting against the modernization project that ran against the grain of both Islamic suspicion of human arrogance and a more general suspicion among the city's populace that the highway was a boondoggle likely to create more traffic at the expense of the dignity and welfare of one of the city's oldest neighborhoods. This drama of human values vs. the impersonal juggernaut of urban renewal had a wide appeal that extended far beyond the Muslim community with the most to lose. The Southern fishermen were fighting to preserve their livelihood, and in so doing, to preserve a balance in nature and among humans a balance ordained by God. The ocean testifies to God's bountiful mercy as "the Lord of bounties unbounded."²⁶ For these Muslims, God's bounties are meant to be shared and not monopolized, a view equally appealing to the surrounding

---

25 See a reporter's photograph in the *Bangkok Post*. June 8, 1998.
26 *The Glorious Qur'an* (trans. and commentary by A. Yusuf Ali) (U.S.: The Muslim Students' Association, 1977), V: 174, p. 168.

Buddhist community, which views greed as a form of attachment that impedes the quest for enlightenment. In fact, in all three cases the causes advanced by these Muslim communities were easily embraceable in the ethos of the Buddhist majority.

2. Nonviolent Actions

Most of the three Muslim communities' actions were nonviolent. The "Mitraparb" was least explicit in their commitment to nonviolence, perhaps because their approach came closest to vigilantism in dealing with potentially violent opponents in the drug trade. But in the cases of both the fishermen and Ban Krua, participants seem to be quite conscious about their peaceful intent, in part because both were mindful of the need to attract support outside their immediate communities. These three communities' nonviolent actions were primarily "tactical" (i.e. geared towards limited changes) and "pragmatic" (i.e. using nonviolent actions not as a sacred principle or a way of life but because they seemed more effective).[27]

3. Organization

All three communities showed a strong and effective organizational strategy. I would argue that being a Muslim community makes getting organized somewhat easier because there are a number of communal functions that need to be performed such as *Yanaza* (prayers for the deceased) or washing

---

27 Robert Burrowes, *The Strategy of Nonviolent Defense* (New York: State University of New York Press, 1996). But see also my critique of the possible exclusivity of these dimensions in Chaiwat Satha-Anand, "Overcoming Illusory Division: Between Nonviolence as a Pragmatic Strategy and a Principled Way of Life," in Kurt Schock (ed.) *Civil Resistance: Comparative Perspectives on Nonviolent Struggle* (Minneapolis and London: University of Minnesota Press, 2015), pp. 289-301.

Mayyid (body of the dead) or burial of the dead within twenty-four hours. The importance of a closely-knitted *Umma* is that these rituals do tighten the community bonds which can prove useful in the course of a civic or political protest or struggle.

4. Faces

One unique feature of these three Muslim communities is the fact that though their leadership are very strong and skillful, they manage not to overshadow the significance of the communities. When one looks at the groups, it is not easy to identify who the leaders are. Although in the cases of both "Mitraparb" and Ban Krua, some prominent members are more visible due to their connection with the authority in the former case and long years of fighting in the latter, it could be argued that it is the community itself that is the star of nonviolent fighting and not the leaders. This seems to be in line with development of nonviolent actions at the global level where the faces of singular leaders (e.g. Gandhi or King or Mandela) are being replaced by faces of courageous people, ordinary mortals fighting with nonviolence against injustices everywhere.[28] This would mean that nonviolent actions are not reserved for extraordinary beings but could be used by ordinary people. To view nonviolent actions from this angle is in itself to empower the others and open up possibilities for more use of nonviolent actions.

---

28 See my "Introduction: Exploring the Frontiers," in Chaiwat Satha-Anand and Micheal True (eds.), *The Frontiers of Nonviolence* (IPRA's Nonviolence Commission; Honolulu: Center for Global Nonviolence; and Bangkok: Peace Information Center:, 1998), pp. 2-3. See also Micheal True, "Since 1989: The Concept of Global Nonviolence and Its Implications for Peace Research," *Social Alternatives*, Vol. 16 No. 2 (April 1997), pp. 8-11.

5. Voices

If the effect of injustice is to silence the victims, nonviolent actions are methods of eradicating those silences. It is not a case of "giving" voice to the voiceless. Rather, it is a case of the previously voiceless deciding to end the silence with their own voices. In this sense, nonviolent actions are communicative. But it is not a one way communication in the sense that the previously voiceless speak. It begins when the previously voiceless decide to speak, speak truth to power, and deal with the consequences while the rest of that society benefits from the struggle. If those who fight for just cause with nonviolence win, that society as a whole will be better off. Even if they lose, that society does learn how to use nonviolent actions and at times feel empowered by them. Nonviolent actions, therefore, are communicative in the realm of power relations because they could alter existing power relations and expand political space for possible transformation.[29] These three Muslim communities managed to emerge from voicelessness and expand political space for just causes with their communal nonviolent actions. What remains to be discussed is why Muslim communal nonviolent actions seem to be accepted as exemplars in a non-Muslim society?

Conclusion: Muslim Communal Nonviolent Action as an Exemplar of Coexistence

In *The Handbook of Interethnic Coexistence*, Gene Sharp, a leading theorist of nonviolent action, argues that ethnic groups

---

29 See a somewhat similar analysis of another concept related to nonviolence, forgiveness, in my "The Politics of Forgiveness" in Robert Herr and Judy Zimmerman Herr (eds.), *Transforming Violence: Linking Local and Global Peacemaking* (Scotdale, Pennsylvania: Herald Press, 1998), pp. 68-78.

in conflict can practice nonviolence while still adhering to their long-term objectives, their fundamental convictions, and even prejudices; such an approach may not "produce a loving society but a less violent one."[30]

It is the less acute conflicts - such as those pertaining to ecological issues or hyper-development in conflict with nature or tradition – that might dominate the political landscape in the next century as humankind grapples with potential shortages of land, natural resources, and water. Such issues are ripe with the potential for desperate, dehumanizing acrimony among nations and ethnic groups. More than ever, nonviolence seems the only path that can guarantee at least the possibility of human survival through such dire contingencies.

Huntington, in his controversial *The Clash of Civilizations and the Remaking of World Order,* recycles the shopworn notion that "Islam has from the start been a religion of the sword" and that "a concept of nonviolence is absent from Muslim doctrine and practice."[31] There are many ways to counter such unwarranted assertions. Some have pointed to the demonization of Islam by Western media.[32] Other scholars have shown that

---

30 Gene Sharp, "Nonviolent Action in Acute Interethnic Conflicts," in Eugene Weiner (ed.), *The Handbook of Interethnic Coexistence* (New York: Continuum Publishing Company, 1998), pp. 371-381. The quote is on p. 381.
31 Samuel P. Huntington, *The Clash of Civilizations and the Remaking of World Order* (New York: Simon & Schuster, 1996), p. 263.
32 For example, see Edward Said, *Covering Islam: How the Media and the Experts Determine How We See the Rest of the World* (New York: Pantheon Books, 1981); and Daya Kishan Thussu (et al.), "The Mechanics of Demonization: The Role of the Media," in *Terrorising the Truth: The Shaping of Contemporary Images of Islam and Muslims in Media, Politics and Culture,* A Report on the International Workshop organized by Just World Trust, 7-9 October, 1995, Prepared by Farish A. Noor (Penang: Just World Trust, 1997), pp. 28-35.

violence pervades Muslim public life because violence pervades world orders, old or new, that Islam as an ideology is subordinated to nationalism, and that it is European colonial powers that have used religion to divide and control Muslim societies.[33] Such counterpoints – along with examples such as the three discussed in this article – help to advance the idea that, Huntington notwithstanding, nonviolence does indeed have a place in Islamic culture and politics. In fact, these cases indicate empirically that Muslims can apply the tactics of nonviolence so well that they elicit the admiration of their non-Muslim countrymen. Muslims are "naturally" prepared for nonviolent action thanks to the Islamic tradition of fighting for a just cause with discipline, empathy, patience and solidarity.[34] All these qualities are crucial for getting organized and voice their claim for justice.

In a non-Muslim society, when a minority group gets organized for a just cause, the majority might not object to it. Sometimes, the voice of a victim is not welcomed because the larger society would prefer to be blind to the pain of the sufferings and deaf to cries of the oppressed. But there does exist those who long for justice, they might welcome the move. However, with the image of close proximity between Muslims and violence, getting organized, challenging existing power could be feared. The use of nonviolence could lessen those fears. If fear is removed, or at least undermined, the act could be appreciated and Muslim communal nonviolent action could be seen as exemplar: an example of coexistence that goes beyond staying together with tolerance or loving one another, but doing the right thing for a better tomorrow that could be shared by all.

---

33 See for example, Bruce B. Lawrence, *Shattering the Myth: Islam Beyond Violence* (Princeton, New Jersey: Princeton University Press, 1998).
34 See Chapter II: The Nonviolent Crescent in this volume..

Chapter VI

Transforming Terrorism with Muslims' Nonviolent Alternatives?

Before he left the village that night, 24-year-old Nabil sorted out a few things. At four in the afternoon he went to see his cousin Abdullah Halabiyeh, who lived next door, and paid him back the $15 he had owed him for a year and a half. Then he cleaned his new car for nearly two hours. At 6 p.m., he handed over a petition he had been gathering to get the local council to tar the road outside the family home and told Abdullah to keep bothering them until the job was done. And then at 9.30 p.m. he went to his bare room to pray.

He was crying and reciting the Qur'an. After 10 minutes or nearly 15 he finished the prayer. And Abdullah then asked him why he was taking such a long time to pray and he said nothing and smiled.

Abdullah watched him drive off around 10 p.m.

> *Nabil's final destination was only 10 minutes away so he must have stopped somewhere to pick up his companion and fellow villager Osam Bahar, and the explosives they would wrap round their waists. At about 11.30 p.m. they walked into Jerusalem's crowded Ben Yehuda pedestrian shopping mall and, in the midst of the bright lights and chatting teenagers, pulled the detonators. Nails and shrapnel, mixed in with the explosives, mutilated anyone within 20 feet of these two exploding human bombs. Eleven Israelis were killed and 37 injured. There was little of the bombers left to pick up....*"[1]

On September 7, 2003, Ariel Sharon gave the final order to an Israeli F-16 fighter plane to fire a laser-guided bomb at an apartment in Gaza in an effort to assassinate Sheik Ahmed Yasin, the revered leader of Hamas. The sheik managed to escape with a minor injury and Hamas threatened unprecedented revenge, declaring that any Israeli who occupies their land is a potential target and that this assassination attempt has "opened the gates of hell."[2]

AFP reported that on the second anniversary of the September 11 attack, the Muhajiroun, a British Islamic group, was planning a London rally dedicated to the terrorists/hijackers whom they called the "magnificent 19." The group spokesperson told BBC radio that "I believe the Muslim community around the world believes those 19 were magnificent."[3] Meanwhile, Abdul Hadi Awang, President of the opposition Pan-Malaysian

---

1 Kevin Toolis, "Where suicide is a cult," *The Observer*, December 16, 2001, quoted in Jonathan Barker, *The No-Nonsense Guide to Terrorism* (Oxford: New International and Verso 2003), p. 11.
2 *Bangkok Post*, September 8, 2003.
3 *Bangkok Post*, September 9, 2003.

Islamic Party, speaking to 2,000 supporters at his party annual meeting in Kuala Lumpur on September 12, 2003, denounced the US as an enemy of Islam and voiced support for Palestinian suicide bombers.[4]

These newspaper clippings indicate at least three points. First, violence related to Muslims will continue, some carried out with Muslims as targets, while others will be committed in the name of Islam. Second, terrorism, especially the 9/11 incident where some 3,000 people were killed with 19 suicide killers, can be seen by some Muslims as justified, and in fact celebrated. Third, given the above two conditions and the fact that there is a high percentage of Muslims who express support for the use of suicide bombing as a method to "defend Islam" in several countries -73 percent in Lebanon and 27 percent in Indonesia[5] -I don't think it would be difficult to find another "Nabil", an ordinary young Muslim, who would sacrifice his/her life for the cause he/she believes in.

This chapter is an attempt to suggest that terrorism, seen as a form of "political violence", grounded in its own reasons yet producing destructive results to all concerned, needs to be transformed into a more productive/creative conflict with Muslims' nonviolent alternatives. I would argue that this radical transformation is possible precisely because of the similarities, not differences, between terrorism used by some Muslims and "principled nonviolence." I will begin with an attempt to understand terrorism as a form of "political violence" and ask not what it is, but how it works. Then the religious edicts condemning and justifying terrorism by traditional religious scholars as against/supporting the tenets of Islam will

---

4 *Bangkok Post*, September 13, 2003
5 The Pew Global Attitudes Project, *What the World Thinks in 2002: How Global Politics View their Lives, their Countries, their World, America* (Washington D.C., 2002).

be critically examined by drawing attention to three philosophic issues: questioning the supremacy of instrumental rationality, the absence of innocents, and the reduction of humans to objects. Then, examples of Muslims' nonviolent actions as a creative form of resistance aimed and engaged to move conflicts in the world towards "truth and justice" will be explored as an alternative to terrorism, highlighting not only the obvious differences, but more importantly the similarities between principled nonviolence and religious-based terrorism.

Understanding Terrorism: Rationality and Dynamics

From 1998-2002, there have been 1,649 incidents which the US Department of State has termed "international terrorist attacks." Contrary to conventional understanding, most of these occurred in Latin America with 676 incidents compared to 387 in Asia and 135 in the Middle East. Business targets have been attacked 1,462 times which accounts for more than 66 percent compared to all other targets: diplomatic, governmental, military and other. It goes without saying that civilians have been the primary victims while the military accounted for only 1.7 percent of all targets. The highest number of casualties in the past five years excluding the 9/11 incident, however, was in Asia with 4,161 compared with 283 in Latin America and 1,462 in the Middle East. The September 11th, 2001 attack clearly contributed most significantly to the number of casualties in North America with 4,091.[6]

Focusing only on suicide terrorism, a researcher found that from 1980 to 2001, there have been 188 separate suicide

---

6 *Patterns of Global Terrorism 2002* (Washington D.C.: US Department of State, 2003).

terrorist attacks, where 179 or 95 percent were parts of organized campaigns with the non-religious Marxist-Leninist Tamil Tigers of Sri Lanka becoming the world leader of this type of terrorism. More importantly, this phenomenon has been steadily on the rise since those who committed them have learned that "it pays." As a result of terrorism, American and French military forces were compelled to leave Lebanon in 1983, Israeli forced to quit Gaza Strip and the West Bank in 1994 and 1995, and the Sri Lankan government to work towards an independent Tamil state from 1990 on, among other cases.[7] In addition, according to B'tselem, the Israeli Information Center for Human Rights in the Occupied Territories, between 29 September 2000 and 30 November 2002, the number of Israelis killed by Palestinians was 640, among them are 440 civilians and 82 under the age of eighteen. The number of Palestinians killed by Israelis was 1,597, while 300 were minors. From the signing of the Oslo agreement in 1993 until the beginning of August 2002, there have been 198 suicide-bombing missions; 136 of these ended with the attackers blowing up themselves and others.[8]

Terrorism as a phenomenon is therefore important to any analysis of the present global trends and politics because it is increasingly prevalent. In addition, the American reaction to the 9/11 tragedy with the use of force to correct the wrong of terrorism has plunged the world deeper into deadly conflicts. President George W. Bush spoke on the second anniversary of September 11th that

---

7 Robert A. Pape, "The Strategic Logic of Suicide Terrorism," *American Political Science Review*, Vol. 97 No. 3 (August 2003), pp. 343-361. The quote is on p. 344.
8 Avishai Margalit, "The Suicide Bombers," *The New York Review of Books*, Vol. L No.1 (January 16, 2003), p . 36.

> *The memories of Sept. 11 will never leave us. We will not forget the burning towers....We will not wait for further attacks on innocent Americans. The best way to protect the American people is to stay on the offensive, to stay on the offensive at home and to stay on the offensive overseas.*[9]

In the past two years after the September 11th incident, the US has started two wars, in Afghanistan and Iraq. With reports of casualties from these deadly conflict sites coming in almost daily while George W. Bush and his Vice-President had been advised not to be present at Ground Zero memorial services this year, it seems the President was right when he said that his "war on terror" was not over. In fact, this war has in some ways transformed the world into a more dangerous place plagued with the specter of violence -where ordinary people are trapped between the deadly force of terrorism carried out by both state and non-state actors on the one hand, and the hardened arms of the state drowning the call for rights and liberties on the other.[10]

If the effects of terrorism are to be mitigated in the long run, the phenomenon needs to be critically construed. It is important to first underscore the fact that the term terrorism itself is extremely political. For example, the US government's policy in dealing with terrorism clearly states that while concession to terrorists will not be made, it will apply pressure on states that sponsor terrorism and enhance international collaboration against it. More importantly, it will try to bring terrorists "to justice for their crimes."[11] According to Richard

---

9 *Bangkok Post*, September 12, 2003.
10 International Council on Human Rights Policy (ICHRP), *Human Rights After September 11* (Versoix, Switzerland: International Council on Human Rights Policy, 2002).
11 *Patterns of Global Terrorism 2000* (Washington D.C.: US Depart-

Falk, terrorism in the US and Israeli political discourse has been associated with anti-state forms of violence that were so criminal that "any method of enforcement and retaliation was viewed as acceptable, and not subject to criticism."[12] However, those who use terror tactics normally avoid the term and claim they are resisting oppression and fighting for justice.[13] But then most governments also exclude "state terrorism" and thereby relegated a major source of violence and fear suffered by civilians around the world to silence.[14] To better understand terrorism, therefore, it might be instructive to hear the voices of a perpetrator and a victim.

In the morning of December 23, 1929, Lord Irwin, the British Viceroy, had just returned from a tour of South India. As he had approached Delhi, a bomb had exploded under his train. Lord Irwin escaped injury and Gandhi congratulated him on his miraculous escape.[15] Gandhi also delivered a speech to a meeting of the Indian Congress party and drafted a resolution denouncing terrorism. He wrote that he would despair for nonviolence if he were not certain that bomb throwing was nothing but "froth coming to the surface in an agitated liquid." The danger of terrorism lies in its internal consequences: from violence committed against the foreign ruler there was only an "easy, natural step to violence to our own people whom we may consider to be obstructing the country's progress."[16] He

---

ment of State, 2001), p. iii.
12 Richard Falk, *The Great Terror War* (New York, Northampton: Olive Branch Press, 2003), p. xviii.
13 Barker, *The No-Nonsense Guide to Terrorism*, p. 23.
14 See for example the data on governments' killings of their own civilians in William Eckhardt, "Death by Courtesy of Governments, 1945-1990," *Peace Research*, Vol. 24 No. 2 (May 1992), pp. 51-56
15 B.R. Nanda, *Mahatma Gandhi: A Biography* (Delhi: Oxford University Press, 1997), p. 284.
16 M.K. Gandhi, *Young India*, January 2, 1930.

seems to think of terrorism as a kind of delusional, irrational act. As a matter of fact, in January 1930, a small left-wing Indian terrorist group founded in 1928, the Hindustan Socialist Revolutionary Army (HSRA), published a manifesto titled: "The Philosophy of the Bomb," attacking both Gandhi's policy of nonviolence and his criticism of terrorism which was due to, "sheer ignorance, misrepresent(ation), and misunderstand(ing)," and that those who committed them are "delusional" and "past reason."[17]

Most of the HSRA members had earlier been members of Gandhi's nonviolent movement, but they turned to the use of violence when their goals could not be realized. It claims that the terrorists do not ask for mercy nor compromise, that their war is a war to the end, and that the mission of the youth of India is to conduct not just "propaganda by deed" but "propaganda by death." It argued that a revolution cannot be completed without terrorism and that it was not an imported European product but homegrown. Most importantly, a terrorist does not sacrifice his/her life out of the psychological need for appreciation or any other form of irrationality/insanity. Instead, the document emphatically stated that "It is to reason and reason alone that he (a terrorist) bows."[18] Because of British domination, an Indian was forced by reason and dictated by conscience to go into violence by accepting terrorism. This is because:

> Terrorism instills fear in the hearts of the oppressors, it brings hope of revenge and redemption to the oppressed masses. It gives courage and self-

---

17 Bhagwat Charan, "The Philosophy of the Bomb," in Walter Laqueur, *The Terrorism Reader: A Historical Anthology* (London: Wildwood House, 1979), p. 137, 139.
18 *Ibid.*, p. 139.

> *confidence to the wavering, it shatters the spell of the subject race in the eyes of the world, because it is the most convincing proof of a nation's hunger for freedom.*[19]

According to Laura Blumenfeld, terrorism is "not so much about killing people as about dehumanizing them to make a political point." She should know because her father, a New York rabbi, was shot and wounded by a Palestinian in Jerusalem's old city in 1986. Twelve years later, she confronted Omar Khatib, the Arab gunman, in an Israeli courtroom and after several meetings, Omar wrote her father a letter stating that "Laura was the mirror that made me see your face as a human person [who] deserved to be admired and respected."[20]

From the perspectives suggested above, terrorism can be seen as a threat or an act of violence against civilians. Construed as a form of "political violence", it can also be seen as a reaction to oppression and injustice, and hence, rational from the perspective of perpetrators. More importantly, the act of terror becomes possible when the victim has been dehumanized and no longer recognized as a human being. But apart from specific conditions, such as organizational/technical skills or financial support for terrorists, it is also important to emphasize three other ways that terrorism work.[21]

First, it works by severing the link between the targets of violence and the reason for violence. This is perhaps the most

---
19 *Ibid.*
20 Susan Sachs, "Punishing a Terrorist by Showing Him His Victim's Humanity," *New York Times.com*, April 6, 2002. Laura Blumenfeld's exploration of the many faces of vengeance is in her *Revenge: A Story of Hope* (New York: Simon & Schuster, 2002).
21 See Chaiwat Satha-Anand, "Understanding the success of terrorism," *Inter-Asia Cultural Studies*, Vol. 3 No. 1 (April 2002), pp. 157-159.

glaring reason why it is often seen as irrational since there seems to be no reason why the civilian victims, directly unrelated to the conflicts, are attacked. The point, however, is when that logical link is cut off; the question of innocent lives becomes irrelevant to the terrorists. The "enemy" society, already dehumanized, can be effectively turned into a monolith devoid of complexities that exist in reality, and thus anyone can be attacked.

Second, since terrorism can attack anyone at any time or place, it successfully robs a society of that precious sense of certainty that allows members to continue their lives in normality. I would argue that in the Hobbesian sense, terrorism retrogresses a political society to a "state of nature" when fear for one's own life replaces a sense of certainty grounded in a confidence that the state can protect its own citizens. When its ability to protect is compromised, if not altogether lost, its legitimacy to exist will be seriously called into question since this protection of its citizens' lives is seen as the absolute minimum of the normal functioning of the state. This is one of the reasons why some scholars believe that the September 11th attack which discloses a structural modification in the character of power and security, requires a different approach to terrorism ordinarily guided by the framework of war with a reformulation of the limits of the use of force.[22]

Third, with the absence of normality amidst the hegemony of fear, it transforms the society that mourns the tragic fate of its victims into a society of possible victimizers bent on using violence against others. The purpose of terrorism as "political violence" is not exactly to create material nor human destruction, though a case can be made for symbolic attack as

---

22 See, for example, Richard Falk, *The Great Terror War*.

in the September 11th incident, but to transform the very existence of the "enemy" society itself into an alienated collective self-facing internal contradictions at the moral, cultural and political levels that might eventually tear it apart.[23]

Treating Terrorism: Muslims' Condemnations and Justifications

A most curious little booklet circulated among Muslims which I have come across has two titles: *Clarification of the Truth In Light Of Terrorism, Hijackings & Suicide Bombings* and *An Advice To Usaamah Ibn Laaden from Shaykhul Islam Ibn Baaz*.[24] As the former Mufti of the Kingdom of Saudi Arabia, Abdul Azeez Ibn Baaz (d. 1999 or 1420 AH) was considered by many a great scholar of "traditionalist" Islam and *Sunnah* (traditions of the Prophet). The booklet has two parts. The first is a religious-based argument in favor of obedience to the rulers. The second is a collection of various Islamic scholars' opinions on hijackings and suicide bombings.

Ibn Baaz called Bin Laden a "*khaarijee*," a member of <u>Khawaarij</u>

---

23 It is interesting to note the militarized transformation of advanced democracies which are increasingly undertaking prolonged military operations that include counter-terrorism and peacekeeping. See an insightful study on the repositioning of the Israeli military in the policymaking process which resulted from its engagement in warfare and other forms of military operations against the Palestinians in Yoram Peri, *The Israeli Military and Israel's Palestinian Policy: From Oslo to the Al Aqsa Intifada* (Washington D.C.: United States Institute of Peace, 2002).

24 *Clarification of the Truth In Light of Terrorism, Hijackings & Suicide Bombings and An Advice To Usaamah Ibn Laaden from Shaykhul Islaam Ibn Baaz (died 1420 AH/1999 CE)* (Birmingham: Salafi Publications, October 2001). The inside cover indicated that it is translated into English by www.Fatwa-online.com, among others.

which was a sect that appeared in the early history of Islam and was said to be responsible for the killings of many of the Prophet's companions.[25] They committed three major crimes: rebelling against Muslim rulers, declaring Muslims to be unbelievers due to sins, and making permissible the taking of human life unlawfully. Ibn Baaz cited a Hadith related by Ahmad and Tirmidhi that the Prophet said: "There are three things towards which the heart of a Muslim never shows hatred or rancour: Making one's actions sincerely for Allah; giving obedience to the rulers (*wulaatul-umur*); and sticking to the *Jamaa'at* (united body)."[26] It is interesting to note that in an interview with the *Nida'ul Islam* (no.15) bin Laden charged some of the Muslim leaders as well as the scholars especially "in the country of the two sacred mosques" as engaging in the major *Kufr* (falling outside of the faith). This is another reason, if not a more important one, why Ibn Baaz regarded bin Laden as a *khaarijee* because his statement was seen as a blanket *takfeer* (declaring Muslims to be unbelievers and therefore make allowable the spilling of their blood).[27]

In an interview with *Al-Jazeerah* at the end of 1998, Osama bin Laden said:

> *I look with great veneration and respect at those great men in that they lifted the humiliation from the forehead of our Ummah (community of believers), whether it was those who bombed in Ri-*

---

[25] Called the "seceders" because they regarded the succession of caliphs after the Prophet's death was unlawful. They later became disillusioned with Ali, the Prophet's son-in-law who was closest male relative and the fourth caliph, for his compromise that one of them, Ibn Muljam, assassinated Ali. See a brief description of *khawarij* in Malise Ruthven, *Islam: A Very Short Introduction* (Oxford and New York: Oxford University Press, 1997), p. 53, 59.
[26] *Ibid.*, pp. 2-3.
[27] *Ibid.*, fn. 8, pp. 7-8.

> *yaadh or those in Khobar or in East Africa, and whatever resembles these acts.*

Ibn Baaz gave his *fatwah* (religious ruling) on "the terrorist attack in Riyadh" by stating:

> *And there is no doubt that this act can only be undertaken by one who does not believe in Allah or the Last Day.... Only vile souls which are filled with enmity, jealousy, evil, corruption and absence of faith in Allah and His Messenger can perform the likes of these acts.*

Then he added his judgment that, "And those who perform the likes of this are more deserving of being killed and being restrained on account of what they have committed of great sin"[28]

Citing a Hadith compiled by Imam Muslim, Ibn Baaz made a point that a Muslim has to "hear and obey" his/her ruler even if "he flogs your back and takes your wealth", even if these leaders have "hearts of devils in the bodies of humans". He also cited the teaching of Imam al-Barbahaaree (d.329 A.H.) who taught that:

> *If you find a man making supplication (du'a) against the ruler, know that he is a person of innovation (bid'ah). If you find a person making supplication for the ruler to be upright, know that he is a person of the Sunnah (traditions of the Prophet), if Allah wills.*[29]

Based on early Islamic history when Uthmaan Ibn Affaan (the third noble caliph) was killed as a result of discord (*fitnah*) among the elites of the time, especially between Ali and

---

28 Ibid. p. 4.
29 *Ibid.*, pp. 12-13.

Mu'aawiya (the fourth and fifth caliphs after the Prophet), Ibn Baaz was extremely antagonistic to the idea of challenging or disobeying the rulers. In other words, Ibn Baaz claimed that discord and open rebellion resulted from "open proclamation of the faults of the rulers". Armed with hatred for the rulers, the people will kill them.[30]

Ibn Baaz's concern could be illustrated by the Sadat assassination. Muhammad ' Abd al-Salam Faraj, who was tried and executed in 1982 for the October 6, 1981 assassination of President Sadat, wrote in his *Al-Farida Al-Gha'eba* (The Neglected Duty), a most important repository of his group's thought, that:

> *Fighting the near enemy is more important than fighting the distant enemy.... The cause of the existence of imperialism in the lands of Islam lies in these self-same rulers. To begin the struggle against imperialism would be...a waste of time.... There can be no doubt that the first battlefield of the jihad is the extirpation of these infidel leaderships...*[31]

---

30 *Ibid.*, pp. 14-15. It could certainly be argued that the ardent support many Islamic scholars given to the rulers in the Saudi Arabia is a result of a specific historical context of symbiotic relationship between the state and religious establishment, beginning in the mid-eighteenth century between Muhammad ibn' Abd-al-Wahhab (1703-1781), a puritan reformer and Muhammad al-Sa'ud, a local ruler who ruled the area from 1745 to 1765. A useful, though brief, account of contesting sacred authority in Saudi Arabia is in Dale F. Eickelman and James Piscatori, *Muslim Politics* (Princeton, New Jersey: Princeton University Press, 1996), pp. 60-63. But here I am concentrated on the rationality of justifications for obedience given by the religious scholars.
31 Quoted in Bernard Lewis, *What Went Wrong?: The Clash Between Islam and Modernity in the Middle East* (New York: Perennial, 2002), pp. 107-108.

When asked to explain his motive, Khalid al-Islambouli, an officer who was the instigator and executor of the Sadat assassination, stated in the Egyptian investigation file record that: " I did what I did, because the Shari'a was not applied, because of the peace treaty with the Jews and because of the arrest of Muslim 'Ulamaa without justification."[32] It could be said that the killing of President Sadat was perceived as a necessity because he was *a heretic (Kufr)* since he did not rule in accordance with traditions of the Prophet *(Shari'a)* ; a traitor because he made peace with the enemy; and *an unjust ruler* because he arrested Islamic scholars *(Ulamaa)* unjustly.[33]

In other words, Ibn Baaz 's argument for obedience to rulers is based on the idea that disobedience, even criticism of the leaders, will eventually undermine their authority, create disunity among the Muslim community, and then lead to deadly conflicts, which in history appeared in the form of rightful rulers killed. This, in turn, would result in the weakening and disunity, if not disintegration, among the Muslim ummah (community). The theoretical question of limit to obedience, a la Aristotle's rights to revolt, was responded with the words of Imam ash-Shawkaanee (d.1250 AH) who wrote that a believer can disobey the ruler if the latter disobeys God. Yet, "it is not permissible to revolt against the leaders even if they reach excessive levels of oppressions, as long as they establish the Prayer and no manifest disbelief appears from them."[34]

---

32 Cited in Nemat Guenena, *The 'Jihad': An 'Islamic Alternative' in Egypt [Cairo Papers in Social Science,* Vol. 9 Monograph 2 (Summer 1986)] (Cairo: The American University in Cairo Press, 1986), p. 44.
33 *Ibid.*
34 Ibn Baaz, *Clarification Of The Truth In Light Of Terrorism, Hijackings & Suicide Bombings,* p. 17.

This formulation of the ruler's disobedience to God, and therefore a justified pretext for disobeying him/her, is quite problematic for at least two reasons. First, it is a highly constricted notion of disobedience since only the sacred religious duty, prayer, is specified while other duties, for example - treating the scholars and citizens justly, are excluded as the basis for obedience among Muslims. Second, it seems that only "manifested" disobedience or glaring disbelief of God would justify Muslims' disobedience. This condition seems to establish the primacy of appearance over other types of "reality", easily concealed in the present times. Both conditions, including the fact that criticisms of the Muslim rulers are discouraged, effectively result in a contracted space of politics. It is therefore not surprising that in the eyes of Muslim assassins who claim to kill in the name of Islam, the most dangerous enemies of Islam are those within and that killing becomes a wedge driven into the texture of society to create a necessary space for desirable socio-political changes. In this sense, it could be argued that even with global-reach organizations such as Al-Qaeda, terrorism begins and exists in distinct contexts where local grievances are voiced. The interplay between local conditions such as the erosion of distributive capabilities of the states, perceptions of corrupt rulers and the power of universal messages such as the Islamic call for social equity and moral piety would contribute significantly to the rise of violent alternative in a constricted political space. I would therefore suggest that to treat terrorism as a purely "outside" or "international" phenomenon is insufficient for a critical understanding of the subject.[35]

---

[35] This is a modification of Barker's conclusion that "all terrorism is local." See Barker, *The No-Nonsense Guide to Terrorism*, p. 120. See also a report on the rise of "religious extremism" in South Asia and the Middle East which are consequences of the absence of democracy, the

The last part of the booklet entitles "The Verdicts of the Major Scholars Regarding Hijackings & Suicide Bombings" mainly comprises the words of two religious scholars: Ibn Baaz and Ibn Al-Uthaymeen (d. 2000/1421 AH), but a short section by Ibn Taymiyyah (d. 728 AH) on the "Seceders" or those who go out of the faith (*khawaarij*) is included. It is divided into sections condemning "suicide bombings," "attacking the enemy by blowing oneself up in the car," "hijacking planes and kidnapping" and "those who partake in bombings, hijackings." Importantly, the document claims that the verdicts reflect "the true position of Islam and the people of *Sunnah* (traditions of the Prophet) towards the evils of those who hold permissible the shedding of blood without just cause.[36]" But it is the reasons given for these condemnations that shed light on the problematic nature of how terrorism is treated by some Islamic scholars.

According to the booklet, there are three reasons why terrorists' actions such as suicide bombings and hijackings are wrong judging from "the true position of Islam." First, suicide bombing is wrong because suicide itself is unacceptable in Islam. Citing the *Holy Qur'an* and a Hadith on the authorities of Bukhari and Muslim, Ibn Uthaymeen categorically states that one who commits *jihad* by means of suicide such as attaching explosives to a car and storming the enemy, knowing full well that he/she who carries out the act will die, is regarded as "one who has killed himself, and as a result he shall be

---

failure of governments to address social changes, and external support and the breakdown of *ijtihad* (independent interpretations of Islam under changing circumstances) within Islam itself, in Judy Barsalou, *Islamic Extremists: How Do They Mobilize Support?*, United States Institute of Peace Special Report 89 (July 2003).
36 Ibn Baaz, *Clarification Of The Truth In Light Of Terrorism, Hijackings & Suicide Bombings*, p. 19.

punished in Hell."³⁷ Suicide is a major sin because it is born out of desperation. In such a state, a Muslim calls for help from God and with patience, God would assist him. To commit suicide then means a suspension of faith in God's infinite Mercy. In condemning suicide as a major sin, Ibn Uthaymeen quoted another verse from *the Qur'an* which reads: "And whoever kills a believer intentionally, his recompense is Hell to abide therein, and the Wrath and the Curse of Allah are upon him, and a great punishment is prepared for him." (IV: 93) It is interesting to note that the content of this verse has very little to do with suicide but everything to do with homicide, unless one chooses to assume that the suicidal bomber is schizophrenic. Splitting the self into two, the self that was intentionally killed in "suicide" is seen as that of the believer, killed by another part of the self that has fallen from the faith. Hence suicide in this sense is seen as taking the life of the believer and he/she who commits it will be punished with a life in hell.

Second, Ibn Uthaymeen suggests that suicide bombings will be acceptable if, according to Ibn Taymiyyah, it is a *jihad* in Allah's cause, "which caused a whole nation to truly believe (and become Muslims), and he did not really lose anything, since although he died he would have to die anyway, sooner or later." ³⁸ Death for a Muslim is not a negative state but a return to the Origin (*Al-Qur'an,* II: 156).³⁹ But these acts of tying

---

37 *Ibid.*, pp. 23-24. *Al-Qur'an* cited is from "An-Nisaa": "And do not kill yourselves. Surely, Allah is Most Merciful to you." (IV: 29) The Hadith cited from both Bukhari and Muslim is the saying of the Prophet that "Indeed, whoever (intentionally) kills himself, then certainly he will be punished in the Fire of Hell, wherein he shall dwell forever."
38 *Ibid.*, p. 20.
39 *The Glorious Qur'an*, translation and commentary by A. Yusuf Ali (n.p.: The Muslim Students' Association of the United States & Canada, 1977), p. 62.

explosives to themselves and then "approaching unbelievers and detonating them amongst them" is a clear case of suicide and those who commit it will be in Hell because "this person has killed himself and has not benefited Islaam."[40] The Shaykh advises against terrorism of this kind because if the terrorist kills himself along with a large number of other people,

> *then Islam will not benefit by that, since the people will not accept Islam,...Rather it will probably just make the enemy more determined, and this action will provoke malice and bitterness in his heart to such an extent that he may seek to wreak havoc upon the Muslims.*

In other words, suicide bombing is condemned on the grounds that it would engender a stronger negative reaction from Muslims' opponents and would then adversely benefit their plight, as is the case in Palestine. Would this then mean that, had it furthered the Islamic cause, defined by practical, and at times quantitative consequences to the Muslims, it would have been acceptable "to the true position of Islam"?

Third, Ibn Baaz maintains that hijacking planes and kidnapping children, which are now encompassing the whole world, are "extremely great crimes." Governments and scholars must try to end "this evil" which has caused "great harm and inconvenience" to "the innocent." Those who partake in these acts of terror "are not to be co-operated with, nor are they to be given salaams to. Rather, they are to be cut off from, and the people are to be warned against their evil. Since they are a *fitnah* (tribulation/trial) and are harmful to the Muslims, and they are the brothers of the Devil (*Shaytaan*)."[41]

---

40 Ibn Baaz, *Clarification Of The Truth In Light Of Terrorism, Hijackings & Suicide Bombings* , p. 21.
41 *Ibid.*, p. 22, pp. 26-27.

It seems that Ibn Baaz here condemns terrorism because of its harmful effects on *the innocents*. But then he instructs the Muslims to dissociate themselves from those who "partake in these acts" because of its harmful effects on *the Muslims*. A question can therefore be raised if the violent effects on the innocents, and not necessarily Muslims who are innocents, constitutes a sufficient ground for the believers to dissociate themselves from the perpetrators of these acts? This instruction of cutting off the tie that binds Muslims in a community of faith because of the acts of terror committed is substantiated by the teaching of Ibn Taymiyyah (d. 728 AH), who said that Muslims must fight against those who strive to kill *every Muslim* who did not agree with their view, declaring the blood of the Muslims, their wealth, and the slaying of their children to be lawful, while making *takfeer* (declaring Muslims to be unbelievers) of them. This is because "they are more harmful to the Muslims than others, for there are none which are more harmful to the Muslims than them, neither the Jews and nor the Christians."[42]

In the eyes of these scholars who condemn terrorism, the terrorists are the enemies most harmful to Muslims because they are born from inside the bosom of Muslim communities. They were made into the "harmful" others, fallen from the ties of mercy that bind members together, and deserve to be destroyed. This last reason is strikingly similar to the argument made by those who are committed to the acts of terror themselves, notably by some of those responsible for the 1981 Sadat assassination discussed above. In the final chapter of *Al-Farida Al-Gha'eba*, Faraj writes that the situation of Muslims resembled the time when they were under "the yoke of the Mongols." He then concluded that:

---

42 *Ibid.*, p. 26.

> *Governments in the Islamic world today are in a state of apostasy....Our Sunna has determined that the apostate be punished more severely than he who had always been an infidel. The apostate must be killed even if he is in no position to fight, while an infidel does not merit death in such a case.* [43]

More important, perhaps, is to see how those Muslims who support and played their parts in committing violent acts against civilians justify their terror.

Mahmoud Abouhalima, convicted for the 1993 World Trade Center bombing, explains that the act of terror was committed for "a very specific reason" aiming at a "specific achievement." Commenting on the Oklahoma City federal building bombing, he said it was an attempt to "reach the government with the message that we are not tolerating the way that you are dealing with our citizens." Following Shaykh Abdul Rahman's teaching, Abouhalima condemns the US because it helped to create the state of Israel, supported secular Egyptian government, and sent its troops to Kuwait during the Gulf war. But in his view, he is against the US and its abhorring policies not because he is anti-Christian, but because of the American ideology of secularism which is hostile towards religion, especially Islam. When asked if the US would be better off with a Christian government, he replied: "Yes, at least it would have morals."[44] He also said that secular America did not understand him and people like him because "the soul of religion, that is what is

---

43 Quoted in Emmanuel Sivan, *Radical Islam: Medieval Theology and Modern Politics* (New Haven and London: Yale University Press, 1985), p. 128.
44 Mark Juergensmeyer, *Terror in the Mind of God: The Global Rise of Religious Violence* (Berkeley: University of California Press, 2000), pp. 67-68.

missing." He compared a life without the soul of religion to a pen without ink, even if that pen is worth "two thousand dollars, gold and everything in it, it's useless if there's no ink in it." Religion as the soul revived the whole life while secularism has none and therefore secular people "are just moving like dead bodies."[45]

The feeling by the terrorists that others would not understand them is quite common. What is not, are the explanations for this lack of understanding. While Abouhalima attributed this absence of understanding to the presence of secularism, others pointed to a lack of shared experience of suffering. Eyad Sarraj, a recipient of the Physicians for Human Rights Award, is a Palestinian psychiatrist who was detained three times by Arafat's forces during 1996. He expressed his shock when a BBC interviewer appeared to understand his comment that the struggle of the Palestinians is about how *not* to become a bomb and that the amazing thing is not the occurrence of suicide bombing, but its rarity. He believed that suicide bombings by Palestinians are acts of desperation, a serious stage of "the seemingly perpetual conflict" after "we have tried everything." He explained what it means to live under Israeli occupation.

Among other things, it means:

- identity number and permit to live as a resident which will be lost if one leaves the country for more than three months;
- a travelling document which specifies that the holder is of an undefined nationality;
- being called twice a year by the intelligence for routine investigation and persuasion to work as an informer on "your brothers and sisters;"

---

45 *Ibid.*, p. 69.

- leaving your home in the refugee camp in Gaza at 3 a.m., going through roadblocks and checkpoints to do the work that others won't and returning home in the evening to collapse in bed for a few hours before getting up for the following day;
- losing respect from one's own children when they see their father spat at and beaten before their eyes;
- seeing the (name of the) Prophet being spat on and called a pig by Israeli settlers in Hebron.

Sarraj concluded that these are why the Palestinian children have been throwing stones, and as a result killed almost daily. When arrested, they were tortured and made to confess. Consequently, everyone in the community suspected one another of being spies. "We were exhausted, tormented and brutalized." He ends his account with a question: "I've told you a few things. Now do you understand why we have turned into suicide killers?"[46] But killing oneself out of utterly exhausted and brutalized existence is one thing, killing others who are women and children, who have nothing to do with the brutal life one has to endure is quite another. How then could these acts of terror which destroy the lives of innocents be justified?

Dr. Abdul Aziz Rantisi, one of the founders of Hamas, answers this question in an interview by saying: "We are at war." It was a war not only with the Israeli government but with the whole of Israeli society. He then clarified that it was not against Jewish culture or religion. He said, "We 're not against Jews just because they're Jews," but especially because of Israel's stance

---

46 Eyad Sarraj, "Why We have Turned into Suicide Bombers: Understanding Palestinian Terror," *Just Commentary*, No. 3 (September 1997), pp. 1-2.

towards the Hamas concept of an Islamic Palestine. It was "Islamic nationalism" which Israel wants to destroy. It is interesting to note the shift from Hamas' military operations aiming at military targets to the use of terror aiming at anyone anytime. Rantisi clearly stated that this shift took place when Palestinian demonstrators were attacked by Israeli police in front of Al-Aqsa mosque in 1990 and the massacre of Muslims in Hebron by Dr. Baruch Goldstein during the month of Ramadan in 1994, while the Israeli soldiers were standing nearby. Rantisi concluded that these were "attacks on Islam as a religion as well as on Palestinians as a people." For this reason, the question posed about innocent lives lost was irrelevant because this war between Hamas and Israel was one with no innocent victims.[47] He added that the fact most misunderstood by others is that the Palestinians were seen as aggressors. Based on the reality of the occupation and the accompanying violence, he categorically stated that "we are not (the aggressors): we are the victims." In this sense, Rantisi thought of the bombings as a "necessary" moral lesson intended to make innocent Israelis feel the pain that innocent Palestinians had felt so that they can actually experience the violence before they could understand what the Palestinians had gone through.[48]

In *Rehearsals for a Happy Death,* Anne Marie Oliver and Paul Steinberg, recounted the statements of young volunteers for suicide-bombing missions in Gaza using some of the data from videotapes. In one case, a smiling lad, no more than eighteen years old, who would carry out the mission of suicide bombing with plastic explosives attached to his body, stated that his act of terror would be committed

---

47 Juergensmeyer, *Terror in the Mind of God,* p. 73.
48 *Ibid.,* p. 74.

> *for the sake of God, out of love for this homeland and for the sake of the freedom and honor of this people, in order that Palestine remain Islamic, and in order that Hamas remains a torch lighting the roads of all the perplexed and all the tormented and oppressed [and] that Palestine might be liberated.*

Another young man said that "what a difference there is between one death and another.... Truly there is only one death, so let it be on the path of God."[49] Seen from the perspective of these perpetrators, their acts are not irrational or aimless wanton violence. Those who condemn it and even call it "suicide bombings" are wrong since it conveys the meaning of an impulsive act by a deranged individual. These acts should instead be called, according to Rantisi, "self-chosen martyrdom" (*istishhadi*) because those who undertake them deliberately choose to carry them out as part of their religious obligation. Rantisi claims that Hamas does not order them to do it but "give permission for them to do it at certain times."[50]

It goes without saying that terrorists grow out of and operate in their specific contexts. But the accounts of those related to terrorism discussed above suggests some common threads which indicate that terrorism often grows out of a context of extreme injustice and carried out to communicate those grievances in situations where other channels are absent or inadequate. People who committed "suicide bombing," for example, are young ordinary men (and women) who made their choices based on their sets of political and religious justifications. What is important, however, is that these deliberate decisions to kill or be killed in the name of Islam are made in a redefined world as a world at war without innocents.

---

49 Quoted in *Ibid.*, pp. 70-71.
50 *Ibid.*, pp. 72-73.

As a result, the logic of exclusivity assumes paramount significance. In the notebooks of some Uzbek students belonging to the Islamic Movement of Uzbekistan led by Soviet Army veteran-Juma Namangani, who attended training courses on terrorism in the Fergana Valley during 1994-1996, *jihad* is considered "a cleansing act" where one of the aims is to raise popular awareness that the enemies are among them. A student writes:

> ...*unbelievers and the government are oppressors; that they are connected with Russians, Americans and Jews, to whose music they are dancing; and that they don't think about their people....We speak of the fate of faith betrayers, according to Islamic law and about how people should distance themselves from those who breach the faith and should side with the mujahideen....it has to be announced that jihad is a necessary religious requirement, for all social groups of people, And in life, everyone must either be a Muslim or a non-Muslim, that is, no one can remain in the middle.*"[51]

Four groups of religious people were identified as targets for killing. They are: "Those who try to gain converts to Christianity on Muslim soil. Spies who work as Christian clerics....Christians and Jews who speak against the *mujahideen* and those who propagate against Islam. Those Christians who collect money for the struggle against Muslims, and those who speak against Muslims."[52]

---

[51] Martha Brill Olcott and Bakhtiyar Babajanov, "The Terrorist Notebooks," *Foreign Policy* (March/April 2003), p. 36. It is interesting to note the subtitle of this article which provocatively states: "During the mid-1990s, a group of young Uzbeks went to school to learn how to kill you. Here is what they were taught." (p. 30).
[52] *Ibid.*, p. 38. See also what some Evangelicals are trying to do in

Reviewing these accounts of Muslims who chose the ways of terror as well as those who condemn them, I am struck not by the differences between these two groups but similarities. What is definitely at work is a drawing of the line between the Muslims and the others which make violence/injustice against them readily possible. Among the scholars working for the state, Muslims who disobey the rulers and become terrorists have fallen from the faith and therefore deserve to be punished, killed in this life and will go to hell in the Hereafter. The world they live in, born out of their concrete experiences, is a world at war where killing and violence can be justified. Yet this war is different because it is not a war between two armies or combatants (a place for non-combatants do exist). This is a war between two societies, Palestinian/Israeli or Muslim/non-Muslim, and therefore there are no innocents. The Muslims who use terror claim that they are the victims and the terror is intended to communicate their grievances so that their significant others will experience what they have been through. These people who commit and are committed to terror were deliberate in sacrificing their lives for the cause of something greater which they believe in.

If terrorism is construed as a form of "political violence" born out of structural causes such as the absence of democracy and unjust distribution of national wealth, and legitimized by religious convictions, among others, trying to put an end to it

---

Muslim lands at present in David Van Biema, "Missionaries Under Cover: Growing numbers of Evangelicals are trying to spread Christianity in Muslim lands. But is this what the world needs now?," *Time,* June 30, 2003, pp. 51-58. It is interesting to note some of these missionaries' prayers. One prays that "the weapon of mass destruction, Islam, be torn down" (p. 52), while the other prays every early morning when he hears the muezzin's call the Muslims to prayer that "I pray against that call-that it would not affect their souls." (p. 53)

by military might is futile.⁵³ If terrorism poses a profound threat to the world, especially in the ways that different people connect to one another with some degrees of certainty, then there is a need to deal with it. I would argue that violence is powerless against terrorism and condemnations are futile because their proponents ask the wrong question. Perhaps, a question which does not ask how to end terrorism but to transform it will provide a more promising alternative.

Transforming Terrorism: Muslims' Nonviolent Alternatives?

Among my collection of newspaper clippings about violence in the Middle East, there is a picture of a man comforting another injured man in a road accident. The rescuer was gently patting the other's face with water. It would not be remarkable but for the fact that the injured man was an Israeli police officer on the way to the scene of clashes in Jerusalem, the place of accident was near a cliff in the Jaber-al-Mukaber, Palestine and the one who comforted him was a local Palestinian. In fact, local Palestinians came out to help all four Israeli officers.⁵⁴ This picture shows two things. First, a line drawn to divide humans into enemy camps that deserve only to be killed is not impervious to crossing. Second, given the degree to which different groups of people have to stay together, it is possible to

---

53 Barker, *The No-Nonsense Guide to Terrorism*, pp. 138-140. See also Jason Burke, *Al-Queda: Casting a Shadow of Terror* (London: I. B. Tauris, 2003), who argues that the basis for support of terrorism among some Muslims is the sympathy felt for the cause worldwide and therefore fighting against terrorism by killing individual leaders or stopping their financial activities is "ludicrous" and will do nothing to solve the problem.

54 Reuters' photograph in *Bangkok Post*, September 30, 1996.

imagine that there are more crossings of such lines than what has been recorded in the press.[55]

In surveying 18 cases of unarmed insurrections against authoritarian governments in the Third World from 1978 to 1994, both successful and failed, a researcher found some which took place in Muslim societies, which naturally involved Muslim participation.[56] There are also cases of Muslims' unarmed resistance in the Middle East, North Africa,[57] as well as the use of communal nonviolent actions among Muslim minorities in Thailand.[58] Some years ago, there was a study on *sulha* (mediation/arbitration/reconciliation), the Palestinian ceremony which is a positive symbol of reconciliation necessary for an alternative kind of cultural analysis highly important for Peace Studies.[59] Recently, a Palestinian academic has written a most comprehensive study which identifies principles and values grounded in Islamic traditional sources for nonviolence based on an indigenous Islamic context which could be guiding principles needed as a framework for the application of

---

55 I have discussed this issue in Chaiwat Satha-Anand, "Crossing the Enemy's Line: Helping the Others in Violent Situations Through Nonviolent Action," *Peace Research*, Vol. 33 No. 2 (November 2001).
56 Stephen Zunes, "Unarmed insurrections against authoritarian governments in the Third World: a new kind of revolution," *Third World Quarterly*, Vol. 15 No. 3 (1994), pp. 403-426.
57 See Stephen Zunes, "Unarmed Resistance in the Middle East and North Africa," and Souad Dajani, "Nonviolent Resistance in the Occupied Territories: A Critical Reevaluation," in Stephen Zunes, Lester R. Kurtz and Sarah Beth Asher (eds.), *Nonviolent Social Movements: A Geographical Perspective* (Malden, Mass.: Blackwell Publishers, 1999), pp. 39-74.
58 See Chapter V - "Muslim Communal Nonviolent Actions" in this volume..
59 Daniel L. Smith, "The Rewards of Allah," *Journal of Peace Research*, Vol. 26 No. 4 (November 1989), pp. 385-398.

peacebuilding/nonviolence in the Islamic context.⁶⁰ The discussion of these studies is obviously beyond the scope of this chapter. But suffice it to suggest here that at a minimum, these studies show that Muslims' nonviolent actions do exist in contemporary societies. Moreover, Muslims' nonviolence is by no means inaction nor passive but has evidently been part of spirited struggle against injustices where Islamic scriptural sources continue to serve as fountains of justifications for them. The question here, however, is in what ways could Muslims' nonviolent actions become alternatives in transforming terrorism?

Based on a specific understanding of terrorism as a rational form of "political violence" and justifications of terror given by perpetrators themselves discussed above, I would argue that similarities between terrorism and Muslims' nonviolent actions do exist especially on two important issues: fighting injustice and death. However, two other important issues which characterize terrorism pose a hindrance to such transformation: the absence of the innocents and the instrumental logic governing terrorism. By overcoming these important obstacles, given existing similarities, transforming terrorism becomes a distinctive possibility.

Existing Injustice

Understood as a form of "political violence", terrorism is a response to perceived injustice, shaped by a fusion of local and

---

60 Mohammed Abu-Nimer, "A Framework for Nonviolence and Peacebuilding in islam," *Journal of Law and Religion*, Vol. XV No. 1-2 (2000-2001), pp. 217-265. See also a highly promising book on the subject: Mohammed Abu-Nimer, *Nonviolence and Peace Building in Islam: Theory and Practice* (Gainesville: University of Florida Press, 2003).

global conditions. This is not that much different from the conditions faced by nonviolent movements around the world, especially a Muslim nonviolent movement fighting against British occupation in India from 1930 to 1947. In mobilizing support from the Pathans in the Northwest subcontinent to fight against the British with nonviolence, Abdul Ghaffar Khan (1890-1988), known to his people as *Badshah Khan* (emperor or king of kings) and to Indians as "the Frontier Gandhi," said:

> *Fifty percent of the children in our country are ill. The hospitals are meant for the English. The country is ours, the money is ours, everything belongs to us, but we are hungry and naked in it. We have not got anything to eat, no houses. He has made pukka roads because he needs them for himself. These roads were built with our money. Their roads are in London. These are our roads but we are not allowed to walk on them... He excites the Hindus to fight the Muslims and the... Sikhs to fight the Muslims. Today these three are the sufferers. Who is the oppressor and who has been sucking our blood? The English.*[61]

The 95 year-old Gurfaraz Khan who had listened to Badshah Khan's speech before joining him, said:

> *...He told us that it was wrong that this land was ours but rule was in British hands... he pointed out that injustice of our children running barefoot and they being in their suits... they could even afford to kick bread and we did not have enough to eat.*[62]

---

61 Quoted in Mukulika Banerjee, *The Pathan Unarmed* (Karachi, New Delhi, Oxford: Oxford University Press, 2000), p. 60.
62 *Ibid.*, p. 63..

Listening to Khan's speeches, many of those who later joined his nonviolent movement admitted that they did not know that the British were ruling India at the time.

> *He explained to us about the British and said how they had come from 80,000 miles away and were occupying our land that was not theirs. They were here to colonize us. He said that we must demand our independence and fight for it.*

Another said,

> *The mullahs (local Islamic religious leaders) and the khans were in the pay of the British so they never told people the truth. No one in the whole Frontier had the spirit or the guts to speak against the British other than Badshah Khan.*[63]

Not only did the British occupy and exploit India, they dealt with those who fought nonviolently for independence with imprisonment, forced labor and sometimes direct killings. One infamous example of direct killings was the Amritsar massacre at the order of General Dyer on April 13, 1919 when British troops fired into a nonviolent crowd killing 379 and injuring more than a thousand.[64] But in Kohat, 1932, following the arrest of Badshah Khan, British detachments opened fire at the people, killing some 300 Red Shirts (the *Khudai Khidmatgar*: the Pathan nonviolent movement in their uniforms) and injuring a thousand more.[65] The fact that these nonviolent Muslims could face the force of violence with nonviolence could be attributed to their organization, strict

---

63 *Ibid.*, p. 62.
64 Geoffrey Ashe, *Gandhi* (New York: Stein and Day, 1969), p.194.
65 *Ibid.*, p.114.

discipline not unlike a military organization,[66] and the strong commitment to nonviolence. This last quality is related to a specific understanding of death.

Death

The terrorists, especially suicide bombers or "self-chosen martyrs," committed their acts of terror for much larger causes, such as the liberation of their people. They are willing to sacrifice their lives because of their specific appreciation of "meaningful" death as a religious obligation in the Path of God. According to Gandhi, humans are advised to

> *learn to love death as well as life, if not more so.... Life becomes livable only to the extent that death is treated as a friend, never as an enemy. To conquer life's temptations, summon death to your aid. In order to postpone death a coward surrenders honor, wife, daughter and all.*[67]

For the Pathans, when Badshah Khan invited volunteers to join his nonviolent movement, he made it quite clear that given the authorities' brutality, death was a real possibility. Emphasizing the singularity and inevitability of death, he said, "As death will come only once therefore it is much better to die for the sake of one's nation and country." Then in a speech at a mosque on December 16, 1931, he added that

> *A man is sure to die whether he is brave or not. But there is a difference between every sort of death. Do not forget your object—your object is to liberate your country. The best death is that when*

---

66 *Ibid.*, pp. 84-91.
67 M.K. Gandhi, *Non-Violence in Peace & War* (Vol. II) (Ahmedabad: Navajivan Publishing House, 1949), p. 338.

one dies the way of God and Holy Prophet."[68]

One of the reasons why *jihad* is so problematic is not only because of different understandings between physical and spiritual *jihad* as often indicated,[69] but also its relationship with death. *Jihad* as a phenomenon has at times been reified and dehistoricized. As a result, contradictions and ambivalence that have characterized its complex history have been erased; and the changing understandings of death as political action that have in part been revealed by history, effaced. Seery argues that this situation is a result of how "Westerners" view non-Western cases of political suicide as "culturally pathological" where terrorists, guerrilla fighters, *sati* (Hindu women who followed their husbands to their deaths) and *satyagraha* (Gandhi's principled nonviolence) are lumped together as "crazed fanatics".[70] In a curious way, a Pathan's choice of using nonviolence against the British is remarkably similar to a suicide bomber's choice because by renouncing violence while confronting the possibility of death, the death of a nonviolent Pathan would draw "the poison of violence" that was destroying the Frontier to himself literally and symbolically. Following Rene Girard's influential *Violence and the Sacred*, his death would become an act that "trick(s)" violence into spending itself on the victim whose death will provoke no reprisals and save others.[71] But unlike Girard's notion, the nonviolent Pathan is not a ritualized scapegoat but a "self-chosen martyr" who chose to take up this burden with full awareness of the

---

68 Banerjee, *The Pathan Unarmed*, p. 151.
69 *Ibid.*, p. 148.
70 John E. Seery, *Political Theory for Mortals: Shades of Justice, Images of Death* (Ithaca: Cornell University Press, 1996), p. 7 as quoted in Roxanne L. Euben, "Killing (for) Politics: Jihad, Martyrdom and Political Action," *Political Theory*, Vol. 30 No. 1 (February 2002), p. 8.
71 Rene Girard, *Violence and the Sacred*, Patrick Gregory (trans.) (Baltimore and London: The Johns Hopkins University Press, 1979), p. 36

price he might have to pay in the name of purification and renewal. Far from pathological, death for a Muslim, especially a good death, is a return to the Origin and hence taken as a next step closer to the End of Time and the Almighty. (*Qur'an*, XLV: 24-26)

The innocents

When a terrorist decides to blow up an airplane or a crowded bazaar, it is understood that the tie between the targets and the reasons for hurting the targets has been severed. But more important, perhaps, is the terrorists' conception of the world on the other side, on the "enemy's side." Rantisi, a Hamas founder, answered the question about justification for killing innocent victims by redefining the situation as a war situation. But even in war, not unlike just war theory, there are Islamic injunctions which stipulate that non-combatants, or innocent members of that society such as women, children and the old, are not to be harmed. In fact, this is one of my basic arguments for the affirmation of nonviolent actions in Islam because modern warfare with its destructive technology has blurred the line separating "the enemies" from "innocent victims."[72] However, the world of terrorism is different. To justify such an indiscriminate act of terror, a redefined "world at war" is seen as a warring world without any innocents on the "enemy's side." This negative monolithic, and in a sense "essentialized" understanding of the others renders violence against them easily justified and therefore highly probable.

My question is what does Islam say when one looks at the world and sees no innocents, especially on the other side?

---

72 See Chapter II - "The Nonviolent Crescent" in this volume..

Would this inability to see innocents among "the others" be reflective of an impaired faith in God as all Merciful? In his sadness and anger because his people went astray, Moses prayed to God asking to be forgiven and:

> "Admit us to Thy mercy!
>
> For Thou art the Most Merciful
>
> Of those who show mercy." (Qur'an, VII: 151)

When Jacob's sons came to ask his permission to bring his youngest son, Benjamin, with them to collect grain. Jacob was sad and afraid the same fate might await Benjamin because he had lost his beloved son, Joseph, once before. Then he said:

> "But God is the best.
>
> To take care (of him),
>
> and He is the Most Merciful of those who show mercy!" (*Qur'an*, XII: 64)

What these verses reflect, among other things, is the connection between God's Infinite Mercy and human's faith in it. Both Moses and Jacob could go on because they have faith in God's Mercy. If God's Mercy is Infinite, will it be possible to imagine a world where there is an absence of the innocents on the "other side" who would not, and will never receive God's Mercy? What would be the consequences of such a perspective on a Muslim's faith?

Here is perhaps where nonviolent action is most different from terrorism. In the oath taken by recruits to be a member of Badshah Khan's Khudai Khidmatgars (Servants of God), the Pathans have to pledge to refrain from violence and revenge; forgive those who oppress them or treat them with cruelty; refrain from taking part in feuds and quarrels, antisocial customs and practices; live a simple life; practice good manners;

devote at least two hours a day to social work; and be fearless and prepare for any sacrifice. But most relevant to the present discussion is the very first pledge which says: "I am a Servant of God, and as God needs no service, but serving his creation is serving him, I promise to serve humanity in the name of God."[73]

There are three important issues significant to Muslim nonviolent action within this pledge. First, it reaffirms God's Omnipotence and therefore needs no human service to Him. Second, it celebrates God's Mercy by the way in which serving humanity becomes a surrogate to serving Him. Third, it underscores God's universal magnanimity by identifying the target of service as the "humanity," an inclusive category. This very last point is significant both theologically and historically. True, Qur'anic verses can be cited to support exclusivity and thereby used to justify violence against the others who have fallen outside the faith as evident from the opinions of those who condemn and justify terrorism discussed above. But the theological ground for Muslim nonviolent action rests on Words of God that are inclusive. God says in *the Qur'an* that killing a person, who does not kill others or cause mischief, is like killing the whole people, while "if anyone saved a life, it would be as if he saved the life of the whole people." (V: 35) [74]

---

[73] Robert C. Johansen, "Radical Islam and Nonviolence: A Case Study of Religious Empowerment and Constraint Among Pashtuns," *Journal of Peace Research*, Vol. 34 No. 1 (1997), p. 59. It is interesting to note that there are different versions of these oaths. See a different version by the 86-year-old Sarfaraz Nazim, a member of the Khudai Khidmatgars, in Banerjee, *The Pathan Unarmed*, p. 74.

[74] *The Glorious Qur'an*. Translation and Commentary by A. Yusuf Ali, p. 252. It should be noted that in other translations, this text appears in verse 32 and not 35. See, for example, *The Koran*. N.J.Dawood (trans.) (London: Penguin Books, 1985), pp. 390- 391.

The choice of action by Muslims, inspired or justified by the sacred text, is profoundly conductive both to the kinds of Muslim one wishes to become, and by extension the kinds of world Muslims seek to help create. Historically, Badshah Khan's Khudai Khidmatgars were different from Maududi's *Jama'at-I-Islami* and Muhammad Ilyas' *Tablighi-Jama'at*. The Muslim nonviolent movement was non-sectarian since there were Hindus and Sikhs as members. It did not invite people to join the movement to improve themselves as good Muslims but to fight the British colonizer. And it did not seek to recreate the local community on the basis of early Islamic example.[75] In this sense, I would argue that this Muslim nonviolent movement fought against the colonizer with nonviolence without impairing their faith in God's Omnipotence, Infinite Mercy and Universality.

Instrumental Logic as Dehumanization

On August 16, 1946, declared "direct action day" by Muhammad Ali Jinnah, communal violence erupted in India. In Calcutta, more than 6,000 Muslims and Hindus were killed while some 20,000 women and children were raped and maimed. Abdul Ghaffar Khan remarked: "I fail to understand how Islam can be served by setting fire to religious places and killing and looting innocent people."[76] I would argue that Islam cannot be served because the use of violence, in communal violence and especially in terrorism, is governed not only by the motives and desires of the perpetrators, but more importantly, by a specific kind of logic. The political

---

75 Banerjee, *The Pathan Unarmed*, pp. 161-162
76 N. Radhakrishnan, *Khan Abdul Ghaffar Khan: The Apostle of Nonviolence* (New Delhi: Gandhi Smriti and Darshan Samiti, 1998), pp. 31-35. The quote appears on p. 34.

theorist Hannah Arendt suggested some four decades ago that the very substance of violence is ruled by the "means-end category" where the end is always in danger of being overwhelmed by the means which it justifies. She clearly stated that "Violence, finally…is distinguished by its instrumental character."[77]

This instrumental character means that violence in general, and terrorism in particular, is but a tool. Its instrumental character is best described by Mahmud al-Zahar, a Hamas leader in Gaza. Following the cessation of suicide attacks in October 1995, he announced that: "We must calculate the benefit and cost of continued armed operations. If we can fulfill our goals without violence, we will do so. Violence is a means, not a goal."[78] As a tool, it is governed by an instrumental logic. This instrumental logic depends more on the specific character of the tool than on the intention of users. For example, if one decides to use terror against the others, the nature of terrorism itself will dictate the way in which the act is to be carried out. Secrecy becomes part of the tool that would govern the user. Small and closed organization is another part of the tool that would make it possible to acquire the necessary C-4, for example. In other words, I would argue that it is the logic of the instrument that governs the users and the ways in which they perceive their targets. Although targets of terror can be conceptualized differently,[79] all share one thing in common: they have been turned into objects, at times through

---

77 Hannah Arendt, *On Violence* (New York: Harcourt, Brace & World, Inc., 1970), p. 46.
78 Quoted in Robert A. Pape, "The Strategic Logic of Suicide Terrorism," *American Political Science Review,* Vol. 97 No. 3 (August 2003
79 See for example Alex Schmid, "The Strategy of Terrorism: The Role of Identification," A report of a seminar in *Transforming Struggle: Strategy and the Global Experience of Nonviolent Direct Action* (Cambridge, Mass.: Program on Nonviolent Sanctions in Conflict and Defense, Center for International Affairs, Harvard University, 1992), p. 65.

a complex dehumanization process which would make killing them easier.

This logic is markedly different from Muslim nonviolent action where the opponents remain distinctively humans. In fighting against injustice, the logic of nonviolence dictates that the user is willing to sacrifice oneself without harming the others who are the opponents precisely because they are humans.

A Khudai Khidmatgar nonviolent soldier, Khalam Khan from Nowshera, said in an interview:

> *We were hit on several occasions but never hit back. I had sworn against violence. Badshah Khan had explained to us that we are waging a war agaaccording to the British with non-violence and patience… and we believed in him and followed him. Once a British police officer asked me why we followed Badshah Khan. He said: 'Are you paid to do this?' I said, 'no, we even have to take dry bread from our own houses to sustain us, and then go with Badshah Khan to oust you from our country.' The officer patted me on the back.*[80]

Turning humans into objects under the governing instrumental logic is also problematic from an Islamic point of view. Partaking in the most important article of faith, a Muslim believes that he/she is created by God, the Creator. God, the Creator, created humans with a purpose (*Qur'an*, II: 30), while humankind "can have nothing but what he strives for" and most importantly, "thy Lord is the final Goal" (*Qur'an*, LIII: 39-42). If God has His purpose, created humans for a purpose and they in turn have to strive by themselves with God Himself as the final goal, then to turn humans into objects is to rob

---

80 Banerjee, *The Pathan Unarmed*, p. 122.

them of their natures as the created with purpose. It also cuts the tie between humans and the pursuit of their final goal, which is God. In this sense, terrorism and violence in general, which turns humans into objects, effectively creates a world where the created has no purpose and the purposeful tie to the Divine cut off. Instrumental logic governing the use of violence, therefore, profoundly contradicts the Islamic cosmos governed by Purpose of the Divine.

Conclusion: Transforming Terrorism?

Terrorism happens because injustice exists at the local and sometimes global levels. In addition to addressing the structural causes that give rise to terrorism, it is important to transform it. I have argued that Muslim nonviolent action could serve as a platform for such transformation because of two important similarities: the imperative to fight injustice in the world and the willingness to die for a good cause. However, two profound differences do exist: the negation of the possibility of the innocents among the opponent and instrumental logic governing terror. From a Muslim' s point of view, both the negation of the innocents on the other side and turning humans into objects cannot be supported by a profound philosophic understanding of Islam where God's Mercy is Infinite and the creation of the universe, especially humankind, is done with a Divine Purpose. Muslim nonviolent action as evident from the examples of the Khudai Khidmatgar, a case of Muslim nonviolent soldiers who fought valiantly against the British colonizer with nonviolence, provide a possible alternative where injustice can be corrected, self-sacrifice honored, and beliefs in God's Mercy and Divine Purpose not compromised. In this chapter, I have tried to understand terrorism as a rational phenomenon, discussed the ways in which it was both condemned and justified by those most directly involved with the act in order to suggest that transforming terrorism with Muslim nonviolent action is not merely wishful thinking. The possibility that Muslim nonviolent action could present itself as an alternative to terrorism is distinctive because profound similarities do exist and important differences could be overcome so that the Muslims' struggle for justice, based on critical Islamic understanding of the world, could continue.

Chapter VII

The Jahiliyya Factor?: Fighting Muslims' Cultural Resistance to Nonviolence

On April 28, 2004, a group of Muslims, many of them younger than twenty, armed primarily with machetes, attacked police posts and stations in ten different places in three Muslim-dominated Southern-most provinces of Thailand. A group of some thirty armed men occupied the ancient Kru-Ze mosque in the town of Pattani and fought a pitched battle with the Thai security forces. In the early afternoon, the military decided to storm the mosque and all 32 men inside it were killed. At the end of the day, there were 106 dead attackers, nine suspects were arrested and five policemen killed in the incident. Some local Muslim leaders said that the dead militants were '*jihad* warriors,' and most relatives of the dead attackers chose not to wash the bodies before burial, a sign indicating that local people considered their deaths as *shahid* (battle deaths in defense of Islam at the hands of non-Muslims) which requires no washing or praying before burial.

Nonviolence and Islamic Imperatives

Earlier the militants themselves were said to have declared through the mosque's loudspeakers that they were doing God's work and they would sacrifice their lives in the path of *jihad* (struggle in the path of God, commonly misused as 'holy war'). A Thai field officer fighting at Kru-Ze told the press that 'they would never surrender but fight to the end of their lives for God. They also said if they died they did not want their blood washed off because they had given their lives to God.'[1] The families of fifteen people aged 17 to 25, who were all killed in front of the sub-district office in Yala, wondered why their children-healthy and good students-chose to die in violence.[2] Though their motives in choosing violence and preparing to die are difficult to ascertain, it is important to understand why violence with mortal self-sacrifice has become a preferred choice to other alternatives among some Muslims.

Elsewhere I have argued that there are strong religious grounds to substantiate the Islamic imperatives for Muslims to fight injustice with nonviolent actions based on Qur'anic injunctions as well as values emanating from the Prophet's examples.[3] It could then be asked at this point, if there are such injunctions and examples for Muslims' nonviolent actions, why are these Islamic imperatives for nonviolence ignored, or generally relegated to marginal importance?

This question can be best addressed by exploring justifications used by some Muslims in their use of terror to realize their objectives, especially their understanding of the historical moment of *jahiliyya* (ignorance) which provided contexts for their struggles. I would argue that there is a need to reconceptualize this *jahiliyya* in terms of a lack of knowledge,

---

1 *Bangkok Post*, May 2, 2004.
2 *Bangkok Post*, May 1, 2004.
3 See Chapters II-"The Nonviolent Crescent" and III-"Core Values for Peacemaking in Islam" in this volume.

particularly about nonviolent alternatives as a preferred method of struggle for Muslims. This chapter begins with a discussion of how some Muslim militants justify terror as their instrument in righting wrongs, based on a time of fighting when *jahiliyya* (ignorance) was rife. Then the notion of *jahiliyya* itself will be problematized with emphases on an inadequate understanding of both the concept of power and nonviolent actions, which contributes to a virtual bypassing of Muslims' own historical legacy of nonviolent pasts. Finally, a return to the original meaning of *jahiliyya* conducive to nonviolent alternatives as stipulated in both *Al-Qur'an* and the Prophet's practices will be advanced.

The Absent Precept and the Struggle against Jahiliyya

Less than ten days after the April 28, 2004 incident in Southern Thailand, Thai authorities announced that a 'New' version of the Koran (was) found.[4] Subsequently, the press reported that a 34-page book was found by the body of a dead militant. Written in Malay, the booklet titled *Ber Jihad di Patani* (*The Jihad of Patani*) urged '*jihad* warriors' to form troops to fight 'those outside the religion' for their religion, Allah and the glory of Patani state, annexed by Siam at the turn of the twentieth century. Chapter 3 of the book tells the warriors to kill all opponents, even their own parents, and to sacrifice their lives to be in heaven with Allah. According to a news report: 'Chapter 7 quotes Chapter 123 of the Koran as saying that: 'You must kill all of them, so they will know you, who have faith, are strong as well'.[5] The Thai prime minister commented on the discovered booklet by saying: 'It's an adapted version of

4 *Bangkok Post,* June 4, 2004. (Headline)
5 *Bangkok Post,* June 6, 2004.

the Koran being used to deceive Muslims....The Yawi version (in Malay) has much more violent content. Those reading it for seven days in a row could go crazy because it is completely distorted.' ⁶'It goes without saying that for most Muslims, belief in the sacredness of *Al-Qur'an* is an article of faith (*Iman*) and therefore a revision or alteration of the Book is unthinkable. It should also be noted that though the holy book is much longer than '34 pages,' there are only 114 *Surah* (chapters) with more than 6000 *Ayahs* (verses).

Seen as a call to use violence against those regarded as oppressors, this small book found in Southern Thailand is not unlike another written two decades ago in the ancient land thousands of miles away when President Sadat of Egypt was assassinated on October 6, 1981. It has been suggested that the major ideological statement of Sadat's assassins is to be found in a book entitled *The Absent Precept (Al Farida Al-Gha'eba)*, originally printed in a clandestine edition of five hundred copies, written by Abd al-Salam Faraj, a twenty-seven year old engineer.⁷ He was later tried and executed in 1982. He argued that the Muslims should first fight against their own rulers who were seen as turning against Islam. Against these 'enemies,' violence is justified, and in fact prescribed, as *jihad* becomes incumbent upon all Muslims. Faraj writes:

> *Despite its crucial importance for the future of our Faith, the jihad has been neglected, maybe even ignored, by men of religion of our age. They know, however, that jihad is the only way to reestablish and reenhance the power and the glory of Islam, which every true believer desires whole-*

---

6 *Ibid*.
7 Emmanuel Sivan, *Radical Islam: Medieval Theology and Modern Politics* (New Haven and London: Yale University Press, 1985), p. 103.

> *heartedly. There is no doubt the idols upon earth will not be destroyed but by the sword and thus establish the Islamic state and restore the caliphate. This is the command of God and each and every Muslim should, hence, do his utmost to accomplish this precept, having recourse to force if necessary.*[8]

It could be said that the killing of President Sadat was perceived by the extremists as a necessity because he was a heretic since he did not rule in accordance with the traditions and laws of the Prophet; a traitor because he made peace with the 'enemy;' and an unjust ruler because he arrested Islamic scholars unjustly.[9]

It is also interesting to note that for Faraj-following the thoughts of Ibn Taymiyya (1268-1328 who died in a Damascus jail) and Sayyid Qutb (1906-1966 who was executed in Egypt) - Sadat's Egypt had become something analogous to the Mongols who professed to being Muslims, yet failed to observe the *Shari'a* (Islamic rules based on law-like understanding of *Al-Qur'an* and the Prophetic traditions) concerning human behavior in societies, both at the individual and collective levels.[10] Failing to observe the rules of Islam in regulating human life in society means that something else other than

---

[8] Quoted in Sivan, *Radical Islam*, p. 127. It is interesting to note here that Ibn Taymiyyah is becoming increasingly popular among Muslims whereas a decade ago he would have only been known to a relatively small circle of Muslim scholars. Compared to Imam Abu Hanifa, his position regarding non-Muslims is much less liberal.

[9] Ibid. Cited in Nemat Guenena, "The 'Jihad': An 'Islamic Alternative' in Egypt," *Cairo Papers in Social Science*, vol. 9 (Monograph 2, Summer 1986) (Cairo: The American University in Cairo Press, 1986), p. 44.

[10] Sivan, *Radical Islam*, p. 103, p. 127.

God was being obeyed. In Islam, it is ignorance (*Jahiliyya*) if a person serves not God but other things. *Al-Qur'an* says, 'Say: Is it some one other than God that ye order me to worship, O ye Ignorant ones?'.[11]

It is through the return to a pristine Islam that Muslims are allowed to realize their destined task of trying to put an end to the domination of humans by those who are seen as responsible for the corrupted order of the world. Influenced by Maudoodi's theory of modern *Jahiliyya* (Modern Ignorance) developed in India since 1939, it could be argued that the influential Sayyid Qutb, an Egyptian modernist literary critic turned Muslim Brotherhood activist, considered the concept of *jahiliyya* central to his theory, since his aim was to show the wide gap between the rule of God and 'that of ignorance', to explain the consequences of such refusal to comply with God's law, and to establish 'an Islamic presence in the midst of *Ignorant* surroundings which are hostile to Islam...'[12] He wrote *In the Shadow of the Koran*, outlining the danger of ignorance in the following words:

> *Jahiliyya* signifies the domination (hakimiyya) of man over man, or rather the subservience to man rather than to Allah. It denotes rejection of the divinity of God and the adulation of mortals. In this sense, *jahiliyya* is not just a specific historical period (referring to the era preceding the advent of Islam), but a state

---

11 *Al-Qur'an*, 39: 64. All citations from *Al-Qur'an* are from A. Yusuf Ali's Translation, *The Glorious Qur'an* (U.S.: Muslim Students Association, 1977).

12 Muhammad Qutb, "Introduction," in Sayyid Qutb (ed.), *In the Shade of the Qur'an* (Vol. 30), M.A. Salahi and A.A. Shamis (trans.) (New Delhi: Milat Book Centre, n.d.), pp. xv-xvi. Muhammad Qutb is Sayyid Qutb's brother who taught at King Abdul Aziz University in Saudi Arabia.

> of affairs. Such a state of human affairs existed in the past, exists today, and may exist in the future, taking the form of *jahiliyya*, that mirror-image and sworn enemy of Islam. In any time and place human beings face that clear-cut choice: either to observe the Law of Allah in its entirety, or to apply laws laid down by man of one sort or another. In the latter case, they are in a state of *Jahiliyya*. Man is at the crossroads and that is the choice: Islam or *jahiliyya*. Modern-style *jahiliyya* in the industrialized societies of Europe and America is essentially similar to the old-time *jahiliyya* in pagan and nomadic Arabia. For in both systems, man is under the dominion of man rather than of Allah.[13]

What Qutb has done was to redefine the notion of *jahiliyya* commonly understood as a historical moment which existed before the rise of Islam in Arabia into 'a state of human affairs' freed from the chain of time, which is antithetical to the Way of God. Therefore Muslims everywhere need to choose between these two ways: Islam or *jahiliyya*. It goes without saying that the latter choice is un-Islamic. Muslims, therefore have to choose Islam and then fight 'the sworn enemy of Islam' to change the world in accordance with Islam.[14] In this sense, 'ignorance' becomes a malady that needs to be overcome because the choice is wrongly made without the capacity to distinguish 'the True' from the false, or 'the Right' from the wrong when human thoughts are elevated to the status of a God. Such a state of affairs needs to be changed, with violence if necessary, as in the case of Faraj and some other advocates.

---

13 Quoted in Sivan, *Radical Islam*, pp. 25-26.
14 See for example Yvonne Y. Haddad, "Sayyid Qutb: Ideologue of Islamic Revival," in John L. Esposito (ed.), *Voices of Resurgent Islam* (New York and Oxford: Oxford University Press, 1983), pp. 67-98.

Philosophically, ignorance is taken to mean an absence or a lack of knowledge. In *The Republic*, Plato explicitly discusses the nature of ignorance (*agnoia*). He establishes that 'that which is' is the object of knowledge; 'that which is becoming' is the object of opinion, and 'that which is not' is the object of ignorance.[15] For Descartes, the emphasis is on the concept of 'error' when knowledge claims are made beyond the limit of understanding. Yet for David Hume, 'misperception' assumes paramount significance when a confused idea of the impression is imprinted on the mind.[16] In Islamic ethical teachings, *jahl* (folly or ignorance)-characterized by irascible temper or hasty and passionate anger when provoked-is antithetical to *aql* (intelligence) or wisdom in the sense of moral self-restraint and harmonious conduct in a communal context. Ignorance, in this sense, signifies 'all that is perverse and discordant in the person leading up to inner blindness,' and is responsible for social disorder and violence. To cultivate nonviolence in terms of character development from Islamic ethical practice, therefore, means to fight ignorance by strengthening intelligence with 'the moral transformation of the personality' through 'a process of grooming'.[17]

Taken together, it can be seen that ignorance occurs when something is understood for what it is not; the world is misperceived; and error takes place when knowledge claims do

---

15 Plato, *The Republic*, Allan Bloom (trans.) (New York: Basic Books, 1968), p. 159.
16 Suwanna Wongwaisayawan, The Buddhist Concept of Ignorance: With Special Reference to Dogen Ph.D. dissertation, Department of Philosophy, University of Hawaii, 1983.
17 Karim Douglas Crow, "Nonviolence, Ethics and Character Development in Islam," in Abdul Aziz Said, Nathan C. Funk & Ayse S. Kadayifci (eds.), *Peace and Conflict Resolution in Islam: Precept and Practice*. (Lanham, New York and Oxford, UK: University Press of America, 2001), pp. 217-221. See also fn.24 on p. 225.

not recognize their limit. All this could result from 'an inner blindness'. Perhaps, an example of such blindness, or ignorance, in terms of nonviolent alternatives could be Faraj's assertion that '*There is no doubt the idols upon earth will not be destroyed but by the sword*' mentioned above. How then could this ignorance or blindness (*jahiliyya*) be accounted for in the area of nonviolence?

The Jahiliyya Factor: Inadequate language, conceptual misunderstanding and historical absence

Crow, Grant, and Ibrahim's [1990] groundbreaking book on nonviolence and Islam, *Arab Nonviolent Political Struggle in the Middle East*,[18] points out at least six reasons why nonviolent actions are seen with some degrees of skepticism among Muslims. They are seen as: preventing legitimate self-defense; an imperialist ploy to pacify Muslims; non-existent in Arab history; without any contribution to the psychological health of the oppressed; inefficient political projects; and cannot mobilize world opinion against oppression.[19] Almost a decade later at a conference on 'Islam and Peace' held at the American University on February 14, 1997, many delegates criticized

---

18 Ralph E. Crow, Philip Grant and Saad E. Ibrahim (eds.), *Arab Nonviolent Political Struggle in the Middle East* (Boulder, Colorado: Lynne Rienner Publishers, 1990). This book was widely reviewed in scholarly journals and regarded as a pioneering work in the fields of nonviolence in the Middle East. See for example, reviews by Anthony Bing in *Middle East Journal*, Vol. 45 No.3 (Summer 1991), pp. 511-512; and Sohail H. Hashmi in *Journal of Third World Studies*, Vol. VIII No.1 (Spring 1991), pp. 346-348.

19 Ralph E. Crow and Philip Grant, "Questions and Controversies About Nonviolent Struggle in the Middle East," in *Ibid.*, pp. 75-90. In this essay, the authors also try to argue against these six stereotypical reasons against nonviolence.

nonviolence as an imported ideology lacking the requisite theological and cultural bases for true compatibility with Islam.[20] There seems to be a kind of cultural reluctance, if not resistance, to accept nonviolent actions as an alternative in pursuing the causes of justice among Muslims. This 'blindness' or *jahiliyya* factor working against nonviolent alternatives is a result of a linguistic incompatibility when nonviolence is translated into Arabic, a lack of adequate understanding of the concept of nonviolence as power and fighting, and a refusal to accept an Islamic history of nonviolent actions.

Linguistic Incompatibility?

When the term 'nonviolence' is directly translated into Arabic, the sacred language of Islam for Muslims around the world, it becomes *la-unf,* which means 'no violence' or 'no vehement irascibility'. The term is problematic for at least three reasons. First, since it was introduced into Arabic before the middle of last century in reference to Gandhi's method of nonviolence, the negative, or somewhat skeptical, ways in which Gandhi has been perceived by many in the Muslim world as someone who opposed the creation of the Islamic Republic of Pakistan may contribute negatively to the acceptance of the term. Second, for those Muslims who are oppressed and believe that violence could both contribute to their psychological freedom from the yoke of oppression and to their political liberation, *la-unf* connotes a denial of the only way they believe exists to alter their condition. Third, since *la-unf* mainly means 'no violence', and not nonviolence, the term denotes not only 'no violence'

---

20 Karim Douglas Crow (ed.), "Nonviolence in Islam: A round-table workshop" held February 14th 1997 at the American University, Washington D.C. (Washington D.C.: Nonviolence International, 1999), p.10 and p.17.

but 'no action'. As a result, for Muslims taught repeatedly by *Al-Qur'an* that '(tumult and) oppression are worse than slaughter',[21] to accept oppression without doing anything can be seen as un-Islamic. The notion of nonviolence is therefore generally considered negative and uninspiring. Hence it is not surprising to see that *la-unf* has become increasingly less popular among writers on nonviolence in Arabic. In fact, a scholar pointed out that the term is for the most past avoided, 'due to cultural preconceptions among Arab Muslims that it connotes passivity, weakness and lack of courage'.[22]

Yet upon reflection, nonviolence can be appreciated as a positive concept, necessary for transforming societies without violence. For violence as such-direct, structural, or cultural-limits life in some form.[23] Hence, it can be considered negative. The double negative form of the word thus renders 'nonviolence' a positive concept. As a result, for those in search of alternatives to violence, several terms are now used to translate 'nonviolence' into Arabic. They include: *al nidal al silmi* or 'peaceful struggle', *al nidal al madani* or 'civilian struggle', *al-muqawamat al-madaniyyah* or 'civil resistance', or even *al-sabr* or 'long suffering perseverance'. In fact , one of the foremost Arab writers on the subject, Khalid al-Qishtayni who wrote *Nahwa l-la unf (Towards Nonviolence)* in 1984 has now been introducing the term *al-jihad al madani* or civil *jihad* in his resent book published in 1998: *Dalil al-muwatin li-l-jihad al-madani (The Citizen's Guide to Civil Jihad)*.[24] It is interesting to note that,

---

21 *Al-Qur'an,* Surah II: 191; II: 217.
22 Karim Douglas Crow, "Nurturing Islamic Peace Discourse," *American Journal of Islamic Social Sciences.* Vol. 17 No. 3 (Fall 2000), p. 62.
23 Johan Galtung, *Peace by Peaceful Means: Peace and Conflict, Development and Civilization* (Oslo: PRIO; London: SAGE, 1996), pp. 29-34.
24 See Crow, "Nurturing Islamic Peace Discourse," p. 62 and fn. 13, p. 69.

outside of these changing academic discourse, a political leader such as Sadiq al-Mahdi, since his release from prison in 1996 and subsequent exile, has been calling for 'civil *jihad*' against the Bashir government of Sudan.[25]

In addition, some Muslim scholars have argued that the terms 'violence' and 'nonviolence' are not *Qur'anic* terms. In 1986 at the first international conference on 'Islam and Nonviolence' held in Bali, Indonesia, the Egyptian theorist, Hasan Hanafi, for example, selected the term 'coercion' (*Ikrah*) to be used as a vehicle for discussing the origin of violence in Islam. But there are at least two problems here. First, if a term cannot indeed be found in *Al Qur'an*, can it not be seriously discussed? I believe that the term 'nuclear weapons' does not exist in *Qur'an* and therefore not a 'Qur'anic' term. But it is a part of human reality with a dangerous potential which could annihilate the whole human race. Should the Muslims be left out of the present discourse for world peace seeking nuclear disarmament simply because of the literal absence of a word? Second, judging from a sociological standpoint, coercion and violence are two distinctive concepts working at different levels. Violence will always be coercive, yet coercion can be violent or nonviolent.[26] This problem is a reflection of a lack of adequate understanding of the idea of nonviolence as power and fighting.

Conceptual Misunderstanding?

In *The Absent Precept*, Faraj maintained that 'An Islamic state cannot be reestablished without the struggle of a believing

---

25 *Ibid.*, fn. 15, p.69.
26 See Chaiwat Satha-Anand, "Introduction," in Glenn D. Paige, Chaiwat Satha-Anand and Sarah Gilliatt (eds.), *Islam and Nonviolence* (Honolulu: Center for Global Nonviolence Planning Project, Matsunaga Institute for Peace, University of Hawai'I, 1993), p. 5.

minority…', then he divided the methods of struggle into two kinds: *jihad* and propaganda. He argued that the 'path' of propaganda, advocated by those who wanted to forsake the *jihad*, can not lead to the desired goal because 'all means of communication are in the hands of the infidels, of the morally depraved, and of the enemies of the Faith?'[27] Since for Faraj, *jihad* meant the path of 'the sword' or violence as indicated above, the alternative he saw as 'not violent' is, curiously enough, propaganda. Then due to the ways the media is controlled, this option turns out to be unavailable and the Muslims are left with no alternative, but violence. Faraj's juxtaposition is yet another example of how the path which is 'not violent' (*la unf* ?) is conceived, and consequently leads to the gross misunderstanding of nonviolence.

In a clever article written in the form of imaginary exchange of letters between Mahatma Gandhi and Osama bin Laden, Bhikhu Parekh has bin Laden presented not as a real man but as an intellectual construct and a metaphor referring to a more generic pro-terror radical Islamist, arguing that for him the struggle against the Soviets was a profound 'spiritual experience,' especially in reaffirming the confidence in the success of violent methods. Bin Laden argued that violence is the only way to achieve the goals of getting the Americans out of Muslim lands-among other things, because it is the only language the US understands. Moreover, for him, violence is not inherently evil but should be judged on the basis of its goals and the results it produces.[28] In other words, violence is a weapon of choice for these Muslims because of its general power to deliver the desired results. Nonviolence is considered without power

27 Quoted in Sivan, *Radical Islam*, p. 127.
28 Bhikhu Parekh, "Why Terror?" *Prospect Magazine*. (April 2004). Originally a lecture delivered at Boston University, a longer version appears in Anna Lannstrom (ed.), *The Stranger's Religion: Fascination and Fear* (Indiana: University of Notre Dame Press, 2004).

because it is seen as a weak and ineffective instrument. Therefore, it is not the language that could 'make the opponents understand'.

There is a conceptual problem with this understanding of the power of violence, however. In a speech at his trial in 1905, Trotsky pointed out that power has very little to do with violence because it resides not in the ability to kill others but in their readiness to die for something they believe.[29] Following the theorist Hannah Arendt, I would maintain that violence and power are opposites. Where there is violence, power is absent. This is because power is not exercised when people are forced to act but when they take action willingly.[30] Here John Stuart Mill's answer to the question he raised in *Representative Government* is instructive. He pointed out that martyrs are more powerful than the authorities who put them to death.[31] In an odd way, I believe that this reasoning would be easily understood by the likes of people like Faraj or bin Laden.

It would be interesting, however, to confront a Faraj or a bin Laden with accounts of changes in the world brought about by the power of nonviolence. For example, nonviolence has been crucial in the fights against dictatorships in Latin America when from 1931 to 1961, eleven presidents were forced to leave offices in the wake of civic strikes.[32] But it is Peter

---

29 See Jonathan Schell, *The Unconquerable World: Power, Nonviolence and the Will of the People* (New York: Metropolitan Books, 2003), p. 170.
30 Hannah Arendt, *On Violence* (New York: Harcourt, Brace & World, Inc., 1970), p. 56.
31 See Schell, *The Unconquerable World*, pp. 230-231.
32 Patricia Parkman, *Insurrectionary Civic Strikes in Latin America 1931-1961* (Cambridge, Mass.: The Albert Einstein Institution, 1990). These 11 presidents were from Chile (1931), Cuba (1933), El Salvador (1944), Guatemala (1944), Haiti (1946), Panama (1951), Haiti (3 presidents in 1956-1957), Colombia (1957), Dominican

Ackerman and Jack Duvall's *A Force More Powerful* which empirically addresses the myth of violence and power discussed above directly. They listed twelve significant cases of nonviolent conflicts during the twentieth century. Nonviolent conflicts were used in pursuit of power, as in 1905 Russia; to resist terror, as in the cases of Denmark and the Netherlands resisting the Nazis; and in the struggles for citizens' rights that occurred in the American South and the people's movement for democracy in the Philippines. The Ackerman and Duvall study seeks to dispel 'the greatest misconception about conflict' which maintains that violence is power-and, indeed, the ultimate form of power-by showing that ordinary Russians, Indians, Poles, Danes, Salvadoreans, African Americans, Chileans, South Africans, and Southeast Asians have not allowed themselves to be foreclosed by their opponents' use of violence and instead relied on primarily nonviolent alternatives to bring about great political changes in the last century.[33]

The *jahiliyya* factor responsible for the linguistic complexities and conceptual myths on nonviolence produce widely held beliefs about the absence of nonviolent resistance in Islam as well as in Arab history.[34] Sadly, due to this absence, many nonviolent actions undertaken by Muslims are not known, or accordingly labeled, and thus the tradition of nonviolence among Muslims has been further impoverished.

Republic (1962).
33 Peter Ackerman and Jack Du Vall, *A Force More Powerful: A Century of Nonviolent Conflict* (New York: St. Martin's Press, 2000). The quote is on p. 9.
34 Crow and Grant, "Questions and Controversies About Nonviolent Struggle in the Middle East," p. 76, p.78.

Islamic history and culture of nonviolence?

The more than 600-page volume, *Protest, Power and Change* is an encyclopedia of nonviolent action from *Act-up* to Women's suffrage. There are five issues related to nonviolence and Muslims/Islam. But most examples of Muslim nonviolent actions from the encyclopedia are only those related to Gandhi, Abdul Ghaffar Khan and the subcontinent. An item on Bosnian Muslims merely indicates their demographic and ethnic heritage, and another item refers to Burmese Muslims carrying green banners during mass demonstration for democracy in Burma. Other Muslim nonviolent actions elsewhere in the world are sadly absent.[35]

In the volume *Arab Nonviolent Political Struggle in the Middle East*, Khalid Kishtainy's essay used injunctions from the Holy Qur'an and the *Hadiths* (Traditions of the Prophet) to paint a picture of Islam in history that is extremely conducive to nonviolence. He argues that violence was neither entrenched in Arab nor Islamic culture(s) and that, like others, the Arabs only resorted to wars when they were forced to. It should be noted that most of the Arab 'generals' in the beginning of the Islamic era were either merchants or poets. Perhaps, Khalid bin Walid is the only one who dedicated his life to 'the arts of war', and is therefore an exception. Moreover, unlike the Japanese Samurai or the Greek Spartans, the Arabs did not develop a warring caste. Culturally, the Arabs have no game of blood. They do not have bull fighting, or cock fighting, or boxing. Historically, the main contribution of the Arab Muslims to human civilization was in the field of arts, sciences and social sciences. They taught Europe the use of comfortable cushions

---

35 Roger S. Powers and William B. Vogele (eds.), *Protest, Power and Change: An Encyclopedia of Nonviolent Action from ACT-UP to Women's Suffrage* (New York and London: Garland Publishing, Inc., 1997).

and upholstered furniture instead of the hard, wooden chair, how to wear silk and dainty linen instead of coarse wool, and to drink from delicate glassware rather than heavy metal mugs. In fact, the world learns practically nothing from the Arabs in the field of warfare.[36]

Kishtainy supported his radical reading of history with numerous examples. Among other things, he pointed out that the spread of Islam in Arabia did not succeed through the use of force. 'The Prophet applied skilful diplomacy and superb propaganda work in winning the tribes and villages. The bulk of Arabia was secured with peaceful negotiations and treaties, and not with the sword.'[37] It should also be noted that especially in Southeast Asia, the conversion process to Islam took place in return for Muslims' bureaucratic, religious, and educational services. The advent of Islam in Southeast Asia was the story of Islam's continuity rather than conflict with previous cultures.[38] Looking back at the history of Islamic expansion, it seems that the Muslims have lost much of what they have achieved through conquest and continue to retain most of what they have achieved through piety and trade.

In addition to Kishtainy's works, there are many other examples of Muslims' nonviolent actions both in history and at present. For example, in 1375, the religious scholar Ibn Qunfundh recorded the remarkable nonviolent story of Lala Aziza of Seksawa, Morocco. The general Al-Hintati set out with 6,000 men to conquer Seksawa. Aziza walked to the Marrakesh plain and stood alone before him and his army. She faced the general

---

36 Khalid Kishtainy, "Violent and Nonviolent Struggle in Arab History," in Crow, Grant, and Ibrahim (eds.), *Arab Nonviolent Political Struggle in the Middle East*, pp. 9-24.
37 *Ibid.*, p.14.
38 Nehemia Levtzion (ed.), *Conversion to Islam* (New York: Holmes & Meier, 1979).

with her words and his faith. Listening to Aziza's words of God's command of justice and the wrong of harming God's creation, the general was overwhelmed. He later told Ibn Qunfundh that 'This one...is a wonder...She knew what was going on inside of me....I was not able to counter her argument, to reject her requests."[39] This is a clear case of the power of words, of courage, of a woman, and-perhaps most importantly here-of nonviolence that could send back an army of a would-be conqueror.

During the partition of India in 1948, there are examples of Muslims in South Asia who sacrificed their lives defending Hindus from the rage of violent crowds.[40] In the last decade of the twentieth century, Kosovo Albanians, some 87% of Kosovo's two million residents in 1987 and most of whom are Muslims, used parallel institutions, a powerful form of nonviolent action, to noncooperate with Serbian authorities. In terms of discipline, strategies and scale, a scholar argues that it is the largest campaign of nonviolence since Martin Luther King Jr.'s civil rights movement.[41] In contemporary Thailand, Muslim villagers in Songkhla have fought against the Thai-Malaysian Gas Pipeline Project using all kinds of nonviolent methods for the past six years.[42] These random examples are provided to make a simple point: there are many more Muslim

---

39 M. Elaine Combs-Schilling, "Sacred Refuge: the Power of a Muslim Female Saint," *Fellowship,* Vol. 60 No. 5-6 (May/June 1994), p. 17.
40 See for example Chaiwat Satha-Anand, "Crossing the Enemy's Lines: Helping the Others in Violent Situations through Nonviolent Action," *Peace Research: The Canadian Journal of Peace Studies*, Vol. 33 No.2 (November 2001).
41 Michael Salla, "Kosovo, Non-violence and the Break-up of Yugoslavia," *Security Dialogue*, Vol. 26 No.4 (1995), pp. 427-438.
42 Supara Janchitfah, *The Nets of Resistance* (Bangkok: Campaign for Alternative Industry Network, 2004).

nonviolent actions around the world, both in history and at present. Once the *jahiliyya* factor is overcome, alternatives to linguistic impasses can be found, misconceptions about nonviolence and power will be demythologized, and more examples of Muslim nonviolent actions will be seen.

Conclusion: Redefining Jahiliyya

The *jahiliyya* factor advocated by Faraj, inherited from Maududi and Qutb, among others, is based on an understanding that ignorance is a state of affairs, and the present condition of the world is divided into two exclusive camps: between Islam and ignorance, the Muslims need to make a choice, and then fight to destroy ignorance with violence, if need be. In trying to overcome the *jahiliyya* factor, it may be useful to look back at the original meaning as it appeared in *Al-Qur'an* and the Prophetic traditions.

The clearest case of Islam fighting against *jahiliyya*, defined as practices common among Arabs before the rise of Islam due to ignorance, is female infanticide. *Al-Qur'an* is crystal clear about this practice in the age of ignorance.

> When news is brought to one of them of (the birth of) a female (child) his face darkens and he is filled with inward grief!
>
> With shame does he hide himself from his people because of the bad news he has had!
>
> Shall he retain it on (sufferance and) contempt or bury it in the dust? Ah! what an evil (choice) they decide on! [43]

---

43 *Al-Qur'an,* 16: 58-59.

Taking the position of the innocent child, God asked in *Al-Qur'an*: 'When the female (infant) buried alive is questioned for what crime she was killed...(then) shall each soul know what it has put forward'.[44]

There are several *Hadiths* against female infanticide. For example, Ibn Abbas reported God's messenger as saying, 'If anyone has a female child and does not bury her alive, or slight her, or prefer his children (i.e. the males) to her, God will bring him to paradise' (Abu Dawood).[45] In another place, Anas and Abdallah reported God's messenger as saying, 'All creatures are God's children, and those dearest to God are the ones who treat His children kindly' (Baihaqi).[46]

Taken together, the 'authentic' Islamic tradition is saying that female infanticide is a violent practice, legitimized by accepted culture of the time of *jahiliyya*. The message of Islam is to stop killing the innocents and save lives by getting rid of cultural violence. The case against female infanticide in Islam as overcoming the *jahiliyya* factor is instructive for many reasons. First, the Islamic cosmology does have a place for the innocents and they do have rights. Second, killing the innocents, those who are the weakest link in the chain of human family, is categorically wrong. Third, cultural violence, which exists to legitimize such an abominable act, needs to be called into question and considered unacceptable. The choice between Islam or *jahiliyya*, reconceptualized in accordance with the moral and historical roles of Islam, would be between killing and saving life, between violence and nonviolence. Using the injunctions against female infanticides as a guideline, choosing

---

44 *Al-Qur'an*, 81: 8-9.
45 James Robson (trans.), *Mishkat al-Masabih* (Vol.II) (Lahore: Sh. Muhammad Ashraf, 1975), p. 1036
46 *Ibid.*, p. 1039

nonviolence is an Islamic imperative for Muslims facing an increasing acceptance of violence against the innocents.

Legends of Chapters

Chapter I: "If anyone saves a life…" was presented as the Nurcholish Madjid Memorial Lecture IX organized by Pusad Paramadina in Jakarta on October 6, 2015. [Some parts of it was first published in Bahasa Indonesia as "Barangsiapa Memelihara Kehidupan…", in my *Barangsiapa Memelihara Kehidupan…Esai esai tentang Nirkekerasan dan Kewajiban Islam* (Jakarta: Pusat Studi Agama dan Demokrasi, Yayasan Wakaf Paramadina, 2015), pp.3-25]

Chapter II: "The Nonviolent Crescent" was first presented in a seminar on "Islam and Nonviolence" organized by the Center for Global Nonviolence Planning Project, University of Hawai'i and the United Nations University in Bali, Indonesia, February 1986. It was later given as a seminar at the Program on Nonviolent Sanctions in Conflict and Defense, Center for International Affairs, Harvard University on November 9, 1988. [From Glenn D.Paige, Chaiwat Satha-Anand, and Sarah Gilliet (eds.) *Islam and Nonviolence*. (Center for Global Nonviolence, 2001), pp. 7-26.] Center of Global Nonviolence Planning Project, Spark M.Matsunaga Institute, University of Hawai'i at Manoa 's and the Center for Global Nonviolence's kind permission for this chapter to be used in this volume is gratefully acknowledged.

Chapter III: "Core Values for Peacemaking in Islam: The Prophet's Practice as Paradigm" was presented in the International Peace Research Association (special) Commission on Peace Building in the Middle East in Kyoto, Japan, July 1992. [From Elise Boulding (ed.) *Building Peace in the Middle East*. (Lynne Reinner Publishers, 1994), pp. 295-302. Lynne Reiner Publishers' kind permission for this chapter to be used in this volume is gratefully acknowledged.

Chapter IV: "The Islamic Tunes of Gandhi's Ahimsa" was a paper presented in the Nonviolence Commission at the International Peace Research Association (IPRA) conference in Groningen, the Netherlands, July 1990. [From *Gandhi Marg*. Vol.14 No.1 (April-June 1992), pp. 107-115.] Its use here is gratefully acknowledged.

Chapter V: "Muslim Communal Nonviolent Actions: Minority Coexistence in a Non-Muslim Society" was presented at a conference on "Cultural Diversity and Islam" organized by Mohammed Said Farsi Chair of Islamic Peace and American University's Center for Global Peace in Washington DC, November 1998. [From Abdul Aziz Said and Meena Sharify-Funk (eds.) *Cultural Diversity in Islam*. (University Press of America, 2003, pp.195-207] Despite our best efforts, we could not reach University Press of America for copyrights permission for this chapter to be used in this volume. Its use here is gratefully acknowledged.

Chapter VI: "Transforming Terrorism with Muslims' Nonviolent Alternatives" was presented at an international conference on "Contemporary Islamic Synthesis" organized by American University's Center for Global Peace and the New Library of Alexandria in Alexandria, Egypt, October 2003. It was later given as the University of Manchester Annual Peace Lecture at the University of Manchester, England on May 5, 2006. [From Abdul Aziz Said, Mohammed Abu-Nimer and Meena Sharify-Funk (eds.) *Contemporary Islam, Dynamic not Static* (Routledge, 2006, pp.189-211.] Routledge's kind permission for this chapter to be used in this volume is gratefully acknowledged.

Chapter VII: "The Jahiliyya Factor?: Fighting Muslims' Cultural Resistance to Nonviolence" was presented at the IPRA Nonviolence Commission in Sopron, Hungary, July

2004. It was later given as Annual Otago Tertiatry Chaplaincy and Dunedin Abrahamic Interfaith Group Peace Lecture at the University of Otago, Dunedin, New Zealand, on July 12, 2010. [From "The Jahiliyya Factor? Fighting Muslims' Cultural Resistance to Nonviolence", in Sentil Ram and Ralph Summy (eds.) *Nonviolence: An Alternative for Defeating Global Terror(ism)* (Nova Publishers, 2008) pp. 131-142] Despite our best efforts, we could not reach Nova Publishers for copyrights permission for this chapter to be used in this volume. Its use here is gratefully acknowledged.

INDEX

Abouhalima, Mahmoud	125, 126
Absent Precept, The	149, 150, 159
Advice to Usama Ibn Laaden from Shaykhul Islam Ibn Baaz	115
Affaan, Ibn (Uthman)	117
Aggression, prohibitions of	35
Ahimsa	8, 26, 69, 71-82, 169
Allah	35-39, 44-45, 47-49, 51, 69, 78-79, 82, 91-92, 95, 116-117, 121-122, 133, 149, 153, 166
Al-Uthaymeen, Ibn	121
Al-Barbahaaree, Imam	117
Al Farida Al-Gha'eba (The Neglected Duty or The Absent Precept)	118, 124, 150
Al-Islambouli, Khalid, executor of the Sadat assassination	118, 151
Al-Qaeda	28, 120
Al Zahar, Mahud (Hamas leader in Gaza)	143
Arendt, Hannah	142, 160
Arab conquest	34
Awang, Abdul Hadi	106
Baaz, Ibn (Abdul Azeez)	115-119, 121, 123
Ber Jihad di Patani (The Jihad of Patani; Malay language, jawi script)	149
Bid'ah (innovation)	117
Bin Laden, Osama	115-116, 159-161
Bin Laden, Osama-interview with Nida'ul Islam	116

Blumenfeld, Laura	113
Elise Boulding	9, 168
Boulding, Kenneth	81-82
British occupation of India	134
Bukhari	121-122
Bush, G.W.	109-110
Civil jihad, Khalid Kishtayni's	158
Coexistence, Hindus-Muslims in India	83-84, 101-102, 104
Compassion in Islamic teaching	66, 68
Christian(s)/Christianity	18-19, 27, 70, 124-125, 130
Death, not a negative state for Muslims but a return to the Origin	122
Death as religious obligation, appreciation of	129-137
Dehumanizing people	102-113
Devil	117, 123
Drug, problems in Thailand	86-88, 97-99
Du'a (supplication)	92, 117
Falk, Richard	110-111, 114
Fan, Haji	33
Faraj, Abd-al Salam	118, 150
Fatwa (rulings)	115, 117
Female infanticide, Islam's prohibition of	165-167
Gandhi	5, 8, 24, 26, 29-32, 46-47, 69-77, 79-82 100, 111-112, 135-138, 142, 157, 159, 162, 169
Girard, Rene	138

Hadith	20, 24, 35, 38, 54-55, 63, 116-117, 121-122, 162, 166
Haqq, al-Haqq (Truth) and Satya (Truth)	79, 82
Hinduism and Islam	18, 70, 72, 79
Hindustan Socialist Revolutionary Army (HSRA)	112
Huntington, Samuel P.	102-103
Identity	85, 90, 92, 126
Ignorance	27, 69, 112, 148-149, 152-155, 165
Indian Muslims	26, 69
Innocents	44, 108, 123-124, 127, 129, 131, 134, 139-140, 145, 166-167
International Peace Research Association (IPRA)	8-10, 58, 168-169
Iraq	9-11, 110
Irwin, Lord	111
Islam, peacemaking	5, 8-9, 25, 57-61, 63, 66-68, 101, 148, 168
Islam, peacebuilding strategies, core values of	9, 23, 133
Islam, five pillars of	53, 81
Islam, peaceful spread in Arabia	163
Islam, peaceful spread in Southeast Asia	87, 163
Islamic Movement of Uzbekistan	129
Israel	16, 24, 125-128
Israeli Information Center for Human Rights in the Occupied Territories	109

Istishhadi (martyrdom)	129
Jahiliyya	5, 10, 27, 147-149, 152-156, 162, 165-167, 169-170
Jamaa'at (united body)	116
Jihad	8, 19, 24, 30, 34-40, 52, 67, 119, 121-122, 130, 137-138, 147-151, 158-159
Jinnah, Muhammad Ali	142
Jus ad bellum	43
Jus in bello	43
Justice	19, 25, 27, 31, 35-36, 43, 51, 55, 66, 78, 103, 108, 110, 138, 145, 156, 164
Kaba'a, rebuilding of	61, 62
Khan, Inamullah	40, 41
Khan, Abdul Gaffar	24, 53, 74-75, 134, 142, 162
Khan, Badshah	53, 70, 74, 135-137, 140-141, 144
Khan, Khalam (Khudai Khidmatgar member)	144
Khatib, Omar (Arab gunman)	133
Khawarij (seceders), war and	35, 116
Khudai Khidmatgar, Pathan nonviolent soldier	136, 140-141, 144-145
Kru-ze, mosque in Pattani, Thailand	147-148
Kufr (disbelief)	116, 119
La-unf (no violence/no action)	156-157

Lala Aziza, fourteenth century nonviolent Sufi woman in Morocco	164
Latin America	108, 161
Life, promotion of	44
Mahmoud, Sayyid	152-154
"Malady of Modernity"	85
Maududi (or Maudoodi), Jama'at-I-Islami	141, 165
Mecca	53, 61-64, 74
Mosque, in Bangkok	50, 83
Mu'aawiya (fifth caliph)	117
Mujahideen	130
Muhammad, Prophet	20, 25, 33, 37, 53, 58, 60-62, 64, 66-67, 69, 72-73,
Murder	16-17, 33, 46, 69
Muslim nonviolent movement, non-sectarian movement	134, 141-142
Nabil, suicide bomber	105-107
Namangani, Juma-leader of the Islamic movement of Uzbekistan	129
Nandy, Ashis	84-85
Noncombatants	38, 41-44, 55
Nonviolent action	10, 14, 19-22, 46-47, 49, 51, 53-55, 81, 85-86, 94-95, 97, 101-103, 132, 140-141, 143, 145, 162, 164-165
Nonviolent defense	59, 99
North Africa	11, 133
Nuclear arms	40-41

Oklahoma City federal building bombing	125
Palestine	24, 123, 127-129, 132
Pathans	53, 134, 137, 140
Partition of India (1947), Muslims defending Hindus	164
Pattani, nonviolence in	34, 49-50
Persuasion, nonviolent	36, 86, 126
Pfander, C.G.	69
Putlibai, Gandhi's mother	72
Qur'an	16-18, 24-25, 33-36, 38-39, 45, 48, 52, 54-55, 60-61, 64-67, 73, 78-80, 91, 98, 105, 121-122, 138, 140,-141, 148-150, 152-153, 157, 162, 165-66
Qutb, Sayyid	152-154
Rahman, Shaykh Abdul	125
Rantisi, Abdul Aziz	127-129, 139
Rehearsals for a Happy Death	128
Religious people as targets of killing	130
Republic, Plato's	154
Sadat, Anwar- President of Egypt killed as a kufr (heretic)	118-119, 124, 150-152
Satyagraha	30-32, 77, 138
Sarraj, Eyad	126-127
Secularism, Abouhalima objects to idea in America	125-126
Seely's *The Handbook of Nonviolence*	70-71
September 11, 1906	30-31,
September 11, 2001	9, 28-29, 106-110, 114

Shahid (death for God's cause)	147
Shari'ah (Islamic divine law)	119, 151-152
Sharon, Ariel	106
Sharp, Gene	21, 32, 46-47, 54, 77, 94, 101-102
Shirer, William L.	73, 75
State terrorism	111
Strike/-s	51, 80, 161
Submissiveness	21, 49
Suicide	10, 106-109, 115, 119, 121-123, 126-129, 137-138-143
Sulha (meditation/arbitration/reconciliation)	133
Sunnah	38, 58, 115, 117, 121
Takfeer (declaring Muslims to be non-believers)	116-124
Taymiya, Ibn	37, 67
Terrorism	9-11, 26-27, 29, 42, 105-115, 119-121, 123-124, 129, 131-132, 134, 139-145, 169
Truth and nonviolence	78
Ulamaa (religious scholars)	119, 151
Ummah (religious community)	37, 52, 116, 119
Verdicts of the Major Scholars Regarding Hijackings & Suicide Bombings	121
Walzer, Michael	43

War	9, 13, 18-19, 34-35, 37, 40-43, 47, 57-59, 67, 74, 76-77, 79-80, 82, 95, 110-112, 114, 125, 127, 129, 131, 137, 139, 144, 148, 163
Weapons, illegitimate	44
Wulaatul-umur (rulers)	116